COUNSELING ADOLESCENTS THROUGH LOSS, GRIEF, AND TRAUMA

Loss, grief, and trauma come into the lives of adolescents in many forms and with more frequency than the adults in their lives may realize. Assessing the depth and nature of their emotions can be difficult; adolescents are typically reluctant to show strong emotions and can be difficult to reach, particularly when they experience the untimely death of a loved one. How best to work with a young person who may have trouble communicating his or her emotions even under the best of circumstances? And what if he or she has learned about the death of a loved one or classmate from another peer rather than from a family member? What about gender differences and the influence of culture and family? What role do cell phones, text messaging, and technologies such as Facebook play in the adolescent grief experience? Adolescents' use of technology creates unlimited access to friends, support systems, and information, but news that spreads quickly without buffering effects can intensify the strength of the adolescent grief responses. *Counseling Adolescents Through Loss, Grief, and Trauma* not only examines these issues; it also provides clinicians with a wealth of resources and time-tested therapeutic activities that are sure to become an indispensable part of any clinician's practice.

Pamela A. Malone, PhD, LCSW, developed the Adolescent Grief and Loss (AGL) group. She is a psychotherapist in private practice and teaches at the graduate and undergraduate level at St. Edward's University in Austin, Texas. Dr. Malone has presented on loss, grief, and trauma locally, nationally, and internationally and is the author of several articles and book chapters.

COUNSELING ADOLESCENTS THROUGH LOSS, GRIEF, AND TRAUMA

Pamela A. Malone

Routledge
Taylor & Francis Group

NEW YORK AND LONDON

First published 2016
by Routledge
711 Third Avenue, New York, NY 10017

and by Routledge
2 Park Square, Milton Park, Abingdon, Oxon, OX14 4RN

Routledge is an imprint of the Taylor & Francis Group, an Informa business

Library of Congress Cataloging-in-Publication Data
Names: Malone, Pamela A., author.
Title: Counseling adolescents through loss, grief, and trauma /
    Pamela A. Malone.
Description: New York, NY : Routledge, 2016. | Includes
    bibliographical references and index.
Identifiers: LCCN 2015037833 | ISBN 9780415857048 (hardback :
    alk. paper) | ISBN 9780415857055 (pbk. : alk. paper) |
    ISBN 9780203699638 (ebook)
Subjects: LCSH: Loss (Psychology) in adolescence. | Grief in
    adolescence. | Psychic trauma in adolescence. | Grief therapy. |
    Teenagers—Counseling of. | Adolescent psychotherapy.
Classification: LCC BF724.3.L66 M35 2016 | DDC 155.9/
    30835—dc23
LC record available at http://lccn.loc.gov/2015037833

ISBN: 978-0-415-85704-8 (hbk)
ISBN: 978-0-415-85705-5 (pbk)
ISBN: 978-0-203-69963-8 (ebk)

Typeset in Sabon
by Apex CoVantage, LLC

Printed and bound in the United States of America by Publishers Graphics,
LLC on sustainably sourced paper.

To my husband and closest friend, Tom, whose support is rock solid throughout all my endeavors, especially this one. To Connor, you are my sunshine . . .

CONTENTS

TABLES

PREFACE

Much of what is written in this book comes not just from the literature, but also from my psychotherapy practice as a clinical social worker. This has spanned over three decades in which I have provided therapy to adolescents in group, individual, and family settings in my private practice office, in both psychiatric and medical hospitals, employee assistance programs, and prison as they processed how loss, grief, and trauma have impacted their lives. My interest and research in this area stemmed from witnessing the impact of both death and non-death loss on the adolescents in my group and individual therapy practice as well as the emotional imprint from traumatic experiences. Many initially came to therapy to discuss difficulties they experienced in relationships with parents or peers, and/or the effects that depression and anxiety had on their lives. They presented with school problems, substance abuse issues, strained relationships with parents, trauma, bouts of nonlethal self-injury often in the form of cutting, isolation from peers, and lots of anger, sadness, and just plain misery. I was initially surprised by the impact that a non-death or death loss had on these adolescents. It seemed to linger and get into the fabric of their daily lives. I took interest in this area and sought to increase and expand my knowledge about loss, grief, and trauma through reading and attending conferences and workshops. Additionally, my doctoral dissertation research focused on the impact of peer death on adolescents. I found it interesting and rather surprising how many of these were traumatic deaths and thus became traumatic experiences for the adolescent grievers. From this I developed the Adolescent Grief and Loss (AGL) group, which I will discuss in detail in chapter nine. The trust that these adolescents and their parents and caretakers put into the therapeutic process, and the depth of their stories, has made this book a possibility.

This book covers the ways in which adolescents in high school, defined here as 13 to 18 year-olds, experience loss, grief, and trauma. The grief reactions and responses of adolescents differ dramatically from the ways in which grief is expressed by children and adults. Much of the literature combines adolescence with childhood, yet adolescence is a distinctly separate developmental life stage. Additionally, much of the grief and trauma literature combines adolescents with children when addressing responses to and treatment for loss, grief, and trauma. Adolescence as a life stage needs to be defined, researched, and treated separately from childhood and adulthood. Adolescence is a vastly different stage of development than that of childhood. Even though 18 year-olds are considered adults, brain development is still occurring. In fact, due to continued brain development, adolescence is now considered to span the ages from approximately 12 to 24 years (Siegel, 2013). The experiences of loss, grief, and trauma can have an indelible impact on the physical, social, emotional, and cognitive development of adolescents, which can then affect development and growth into adulthood. Given this premise, it is important to focus not only on loss, grief, and trauma that occurs during adolescence but also on the needs of adolescents as they make their way through the emotional labyrinth dealing with these various experiences.

Chapter one is on adolescent development with a focus on the four domains of physical, social, emotional, and cognitive development. It divides adolescence into two distinct phases, of early adolescence as ages 10 to 14 and late adolescence as ages 15 to 18. Furthermore, it delineates the effects of these four domains on each of these phases. The complexities of adolescent brain development are explored.

Chapter two explains the nature of adolescent loss, grief, and trauma, exploring how it is distinctly different from the loss, grief, and trauma experienced by children or adults. Adolescent loss, grief, and trauma also differs from the loss, grief, and trauma of emerging adults ages 18 to 25. Throughout this chapter you will hear the voices of adolescents as they describe their loss, grief, and trauma experiences via the four domains of physical, social, emotional, and cognitive loss, grief, and trauma responses. The concept of disenfranchised grief is examined as it relates to adolescents.

Chapter three explores some of the non-death losses that occur in the lives of adolescents to include parental divorce, the incarceration of a parent, the relocation from one city to another or even state or country due to a myriad of reasons, the pain involved in the loss of a friendship, and the inevitable impact of a romantic breakup.

Chapter four looks closely at the death of loved ones and others in the lives of adolescents. Included with the death of family members are the deaths of friends or peers, and pets. Additionally, death that occurs in the school setting is discussed.

Chapter five delineates the differences between adolescent girls' relationships and adolescent boys' relationships, which influence how they react and respond to loss, grief, and trauma. The feelings may be similar yet the ways in which each gender expresses them can vary. More important than gender itself is differing grief styles, such as intuitive and instrumental ways of grieving, which may or may not align with gender (Doka & Martin, 2010).

Chapter six explains what grieving adolescents need in terms of connection with and support from adults and family members, friends and peers, and the school and community. The importance and necessity of psychoeducation is explained with a focus on the vocabulary of loss, grief, and trauma, as well as details regarding the teaching and use of symptom management and reduction.

Chapter seven involves the use and impact of technology and social media. Adolescents are digital natives in that they have grown up with and are comfortable utilizing technology and social media in ways that may differ greatly from the world of their parents and teachers, who are predominantly digital immigrants. Both the benefits and the risks of technology and social media use are discussed. The concept of continuing bonds is explained and how adolescents evidence their need for this via their use of Facebook as a virtual grave marker.

Chapter eight supports the idea that adolescents do well in group therapy when dealing with loss, grief, and trauma. Coed versus gender-specific groups are discussed as well as the various settings in which adolescent groups occur. Examples of group activities are provided.

Chapter nine outlines the Adolescent Grief and Loss (AGL) group, its structure, rationale, and the specific tasks involved in each group session.

Chapter ten focuses on a variety of therapeutic activities, counseling methods, and techniques that I have found to be useful in working with adolescents experiencing loss, grief, and trauma situations. Case examples are given for each therapeutic activity as a way of underscoring its power and effectiveness. Given that the nature of loss, grief, and trauma in adolescence differs from that of children and adults, so too do therapeutic approaches.

Woven throughout this book are the concepts of both disenfranchised grief and continuing bonds. Many times adolescents are the forgotten grievers who experience disenfranchisement as their loss, grief, and trauma responses are minimized, discounted, or just unrecognized. Continuing bonds is an imperative concept and method of maintaining connection to the deceased. It will be illustrated how this is positive, normal, and life affirming for many adolescents. Please keep in mind that the majority of adolescents are resilient and, if provided support, nurturance, and understanding, find meaning and purpose as they move beyond the experience of loss, grief, and trauma.

CHAPTER 1

Adolescent Development

What is adolescence? There are multiple definitions for this stage of life. It is often referred to as a time of turbulence, storm, hormonal rage, and emotional fluctuation. This can be true, but it is also a transitional period of physical, social, emotional, and cognitive development that involves change, growth, and learning about oneself in relation to others as well as to one's environment. These changes can present exciting possibilities as adolescents learn about themselves. The events and experiences that occur during adolescence help to lay important groundwork for the growth and development involved as they head toward adulthood. Trial and error is often the norm where adolescents get to try out who they are and who they are becoming. They do this with peers, friends, classmates, teachers and coaches, parents/guardians, and extended family members. This trying out of self can be subtle or blatant, calm or stormy, and most certainly involves a degree of confusion for both the adolescent and the adults in his life. The hope is that out of this chaos comes some clarity. This is an important period for the formation of self-esteem, determination of self-efficacy, absorption of others' perceptions, and acquisition of the ability to manage life demands and unexpected change (Steese, Dollette, Phillips, Hossfeld, Matthews, & Taormina, 2006).

Given this time of transformative growth, it is important to understand that the loss, grief, and trauma that adolescents experience must be viewed from the perspective of a developmental framework. When these experiences occur, they can make an indelible mark on an adolescent's development, which may and often does carry into adulthood. How an adolescent navigates the impact of loss, grief, and trauma will undeniably shape and determine how she handles her inevitable future experiences with loss, grief, and trauma. No one escapes experiencing loss, grief, and some amount of trauma.

Adolescence can be defined by early adolescence, late adolescence, and emerging adulthood. There is not general consensus regarding the age ranges of each of these phases, but for the purposes of this book early adolescence is defined as between the ages of 10 and 14 years, late adolescence between the ages of 15 and 18 years, and emerging adulthood as between the ages of 18 and 25 years (Arnett, 2006). However, this book considers the 18 year-olds who are still in high school as adolescents rather than emerging adults. To further complicate the definition of when adolescence is complete, neuroscientists define this period as extending until approximately 25 years of age due to the still developing structure of the brain (Dahl & Spear, 2004). This is when the prefrontal cortex, which controls emotional self-regulation, emotional responses and behaviors, and impacts problem-solving abilities, is completely developed (Dahl & Spear, 2004). Brain development is delicately unfolding as adolescents gain new experiences, learn new skills, and make decisions in their daily lives. The plasticity, or continuation, of adolescent brain development has interesting implications for the impact of loss, grief, and trauma as well as the effects of repair and resolution achieved through the process of therapy and the utilization of developmentally appropriate therapeutic techniques.

There is a complex intersection between the normative, developmental tasks in adolescence and the specific, situational tasks involved in coping with loss, grief, and trauma (Corr & Balk, 1996). It is important, therefore, to consider the developmental tasks inherent in both early and late adolescence. It is also imperative to recognize that there are individual variances in each of these developmental time periods. Additionally, adolescence can be viewed as composed of four distinct developmental domains that include physical development, social development, emotional development, and cognitive development. The fundamental tasks inherently involved in each of these developmental domains lead to identity formation as adolescents prepare for and enter into adulthood. Each of these will be explained and explored in detail, including the dramatic growth in neurodevelopment that occurs in adolescence, to provide a framework within which to place the experience of adolescent loss, grief, and trauma.

EARLY ADOLESCENCE

This developmental stage of adolescence is defined as between the ages of 10 and 14 years (Arnett, 2006). Since this book focuses on adolescents in high school, early adolescence includes 13 and 14 year-olds who are typically in 9th grade. In discussing the domains of physical, social, emotional, and cognitive development, it is important to keep in mind that an adolescent can appear to be further along in some aspects of these developmental domains while behind in others. Not all adolescents develop at the same rate. For example, a 14 year-old girl may physically appear older than her chronological years, giving the impression of a sense of sophistication that she does not possess until her social, emotional, and cognitive development catches up at around the age of 17. This pseudo-sophistication can be confusing to the adults in her life who may expect her behavior to match her appearance.

Physical Development During Early Adolescence

During adolescence, the body changes dramatically. The physical development of this age group includes the biological changes inherent in puberty such as reaching what for most becomes their adult height and weight. Many adolescents evidence a growth spurt during early adolescence when girls experience the development of breasts, and facial hair begins appearing on boys. At this point they are certainly biologically capable of having babies. Boys tend to lag behind girls in attaining height during early adolescence but usually become taller later on. Physical clumsiness and awkwardness may accompany this growth spurt as the adolescent brain adjusts to an increased body size and longer arms and legs. Some adolescent bodies can appear disproportionate until all parts catch up with one another and even out. This is the point in time when the gawky boy has seemingly overnight become a handsome young man. Although many adolescents may seem adult in physique and appearance, as mentioned previously, they are still under development socially, emotionally, and cognitively.

Social Development During Early Adolescence

The social world of early adolescence may differ dramatically from that of childhood. With the transition from middle school to high school comes the possibility of forming a larger social network. This includes classmates, both male and female, as well as parents, teachers, coaches, and other school personnel. The world of age-mates and adults expands greatly. Exposure to diverse ethnic, racial, religious, sexuality, gender identity, and socioeconomic backgrounds also increases. The world becomes a much larger place as adolescents move beyond their family of origin and smaller world of the middle school years.

Peers become extremely important in the world of the adolescent. Parents may feel somewhat displaced as their 14 year-old daughter focuses on the need for connection among her peer group and places more importance on time with her friends than with her family. She also places more weight and importance on the advice of friends than that of her parents. Many adolescents spend much time developing positive friendships that can provide them support, feedback, intimacy, loyalty, and trust. The development and maintenance of peer relationships is an important developmental task of adolescence that allows them to develop interpersonal competence as they find ways to both fit in and to stand out. The relationship characteristic of the middle school tween and the 9th grade teen shifts dramatically from one that was predominantly family-focused to one that can appear almost exclusively friend-focused. She desperately wants to fit in with her peers yet also wants to be her own independent person. She wants to make her own decisions but still needs to and must depend on her parents for feedback and approval in making those same decisions.

Emotional Development During Early Adolescence

Early adolescents also begin a critical scrutiny of their parents and the other significant adults in their lives. They begin to strive for independence, wanting to make their own decisions, yet must rely on their parents for transportation, food, clothing, finances, and feedback and opinions about those very decisions. Early adolescence involves developing autonomy from parents and the forging of a more distinctive, mature identity, with skills gained at being independent and self-governing (Balk & Corr, 1996). This can be a time of confusion as parents begin to allow room for their early adolescent's desire for independence while also still having to do battle with him to complete his chores and follow through on decisions made, and yet needing to step in as he argues with siblings. Yet, as an early adolescent, he still needs family support as he builds his emerging sense of self. Fleming and Balmer (1996) summarize this developmental period as a phase of conflict regarding independence versus dependence, as described by the push-pull of mixed messages that parents receive from their early adolescent.

Cognitive Development During Early Adolescence

Most early adolescents think in concrete terms where they perceive things as right or wrong, good or bad, black or white, exquisitely wonderful or earth-shatteringly awful. They are very focused on the present, which explains why early adolescents have great difficulty understanding the future consequences of their current actions. However, this is the beginning of a gain in perspective where adolescents realize that information and experiences can be interpreted in different ways. They begin to understand that their reactions to and thoughts about events may actually differ from that of a friend or family member. This can be especially useful when helping early adolescents process through thoughts, feelings, and behavior related to loss, grief, and trauma experiences. The early adolescence of 9th and some 10th graders marks an advance in abstract thinking and an increased capacity for problem solving (Noppe & Noppe, 2004). This age group is able to move beyond the typical self-scrutiny of adolescence to see others' perspectives, with a tendency to give more value to the ideas and opinions of their peers (Balk, 1996). There is a decline in absolute thinking, with a beginning ability to tolerate shades of gray and uncertainty as well as to reflect on their own and others' experiences.

LATE ADOLESCENCE

This developmental stage of adolescence is defined as between the ages of 15 and 18 years (Arnett, 2006), which encompasses the majority of high school students, typically those in 10th, 11th, and 12th grades. Late adolescence is marked by many life changes that cause both exhilaration and anxiety for 11th and 12th graders. The accumulation of past successes and failures contributes to the sense of expectancy about the future, and a more stable character formation has been achieved (Noppe & Noppe, 1997). It is easier at this point in time to recognize and define an adolescent's personality and temperament. Late adolescence is a time when forming and maintaining meaningful intimate and committed relationships is prized. Fleming and Balmer (1996) summarize late adolescence as a phase of closeness versus distance. This is witnessed in their changing relationship with parents and siblings as well as with friends and peers. Many parents describe a sense of push-pull where their adolescent lets them in one day and shuts them out the next. The evolving maturity during late adolescence tends to eliminate denial as an ongoing coping strategy, which then creates more psychological distress than is typically reported by younger adolescents (Balk, 1996). The reality of good and bad grades, positive and negative friendship aspects, and their true abilities dominate their perspective.

Physical Development During Late Adolescence

Physically, most in late adolescence have completed puberty, and many have achieved their full adult height. There is less variation in physical and sexual growth characteristics between males and females as well as between groups of males, and between groups of females. Those adolescents who developed secondary sex characteristics early now finally fit in with everyone else, and those adolescents who developed late have mostly caught up with the majority of their peers by the later years of adolescence. During late adolescence, many are adjusting to their sexually maturing bodies and feelings, and may be drawn toward more intimate and romantic relationships. At the same time, adolescents are establishing a sexual identity, whether heterosexual, gay, lesbian, bisexual, or transgender, and are learning the skills inherent in developing and maintaining a romantic relationship (Choate, 2014).

Social Development During Late Adolescence

During late adolescence, ages 15 to 18, the preference is to spend time with peers, which tends to take precedence over time spent with family. The world of the adolescent is a very relational world that is dominated by the peer group (Noppe & Noppe, 2004). They want to be around others their same age and in their same grade. The major task of adolescence is identity formation, with themes of separation and connectedness having primacy. Identity tends to shift away from parents and family, although attachment to parents is still vital, and move toward forming identity among peers (Noppe & Noppe, 2004). Instead of relying on parents and other family members for acceptance and approval, they turn to friends and peers for reflection of worth. Peer relationships are extremely important and help to shape the emotional, social, and cognitive development of each adolescent, playing a central role in an adolescent's developing ability to deal with various psychosocial tasks (Oltjenbruns, 1996). Adolescents have the opportunity to practice who they are and who they might become. The growth of friendship involves characteristics that include an acceptance of one another, a sense of loyalty and commitment, the possibility of intimacy, reinforcement of ego, and a mutual helping of one another (Oltjenbruns, 1996). Late adolescents who struggle with developing friendship and peer networks often experience loneliness and an unsure sense of self. This is an important period for the formation of self-esteem, determination of self-efficacy, absorption of others' perceptions, and acquisition of the ability to manage life demands and unexpected change (Steese et al., 2006). Adolescents perceive themselves as members of the peer culture and view their peers, popular culture, and themselves as the support system that offers feedback and definition about who they are and who they are becoming. There is absorption with sameness and difference among peers. They want to belong, yet they do not want to be viewed as just like everyone else. An adolescent's peer group reflects who he or she is developing into, as adolescents tend to attract and join groups of peers who share the same values, attitudes, and behaviors. The development of both male and female friendships becomes more common in late adolescence, with more acceptance regarding differences. This is a time when antisocial peer groups can influence and increase an adolescent's antisocial behavior, such as substance use and abuse, skipping school, and getting into legal trouble.

Building onto the early adolescent's burgeoning realization that there are different reactions to and thoughts about life experiences, late adolescents begin to accept their parents' or other adults' perspectives. Late adolescents have the ability to think abstractly, and not just accept others' perspectives but understand them as well. They begin to apply this skill to manage conflicts and problems in their relationships with both friends and family. They also begin to question others' ideas and to develop their own perspectives, thoughts, and opinions based on their life experiences up to this point in time.

Often parents notice that conflicts begin to decrease with late adolescents who have begun to recognize parents as individuals. Adolescents need and may want to find a balance between time spent with peers and time spent with parents and other adults in their lives. They begin to value these adults' perspectives and opinions, at times asking for feedback but still wanting to make their own decisions. Many late adolescents show an increase in responsible behaviors such as cooking a meal, buying their own clothing, doing their own laundry, and handling some of their own finances.

Emotional Development During Late Adolescence

Physically and socially, adolescents may display a pseudosophistication that does not correspond with their emotional age. Brain development during late adolescence continues to be uneven yet evidences plasticity, which allows for the beginning of emotional regulation. However, adolescents still need mature adults with whom to connect in order to assist with mood regulation and impulse control (Siegel, 1999). Adult involvement is imperative in guiding and supporting them through emotionally challenging situations for learning how to solve problems and to effectively cope. Consistent assistance in the provision of comforting responses during loss, grief, and trauma helps adolescents internalize empathy and caring. This leads them to develop the ability to provide these important characteristics for themselves. Basically, they gain the ability to understand and identify their own emotional landscape, to begin to use specific feeling words to explain their emotional experiences, and to self-soothe in healthy ways. As late adolescents mature, they can better identify complex emotions and in turn understand the emotions of their friends and family members. This newly developing skill allows adolescents to explain and explore the thoughts and feelings related to their loss, grief, and trauma experience, and to insight and understanding, to obtain clarity from the chaos.

Again, this can be a confusing time due to the late adolescent's need to assert his independence, when he tends to distance himself from parents. His developing autonomy may take many forms; he may be less overtly affectionate, certainly prefer time spent with friends over family, push the limits of parental authority, and challenge the rules. At the same time, he may seek out and crave attention and feedback from parents. This can be a confusing time for parents when the late adolescent still needs the safety and security of their support and understanding while trying out this new sense of self.

Cognitive Development During Late Adolescence

By late adolescence, there exists the ability to think abstractly and hypothetically, and to perceive the subtleties of situations and ideas. Despite an adolescent's natural narcissism and preference for living and acting impulsively in the moment, she possesses an awareness of the future. The process of identify formation is intense as she experiments with different roles in regards to dress, styles, sexuality, values, friendships, and especially conceptualizing future plans. This is evident from her fluctuation between dreams and reality regarding college, jobs/professions, and where she might live. She has also gained the capacity to think deeply and to solve complex problems.

Awareness involves observation, objectivity, and openness, which is the culmination of complete development of the prefrontal cortex (Siegel, 2011). Observation is the ability that an adolescent develops to perceive herself as she experiences an event. This self-observation allows her to view the larger context in which she is living, and offers her the opportunity to "disengage from automatic behaviors and habitual responses" (Siegel, 2011, p. 32). She develops an ability to comprehend another person's perspective and to see the bigger societal picture. When an adolescent gains objectivity, it allows her to experience thoughts and feelings but not become overwhelmed by them. She develops discernment, the ability to "see that a thought or feeling is just mental activity, not absolute reality" (Siegel, 2011, p. 32). Openness is the ability to be receptive to thoughts, feelings, and experiences, and to let go of assumptions. This is evident when an adolescent recognizes judgments and expectations that may limit her awareness of herself (Siegel, 2011). We begin to see glimmers of this in late adolescence when there is an increased ability to empathize with others. There is a downside to this greater capacity for self-reflection, increased empathy, and new interest in societal issues. It may cause increased vulnerability to worrying, depression, and concern for others' opinions, especially among girls (Choate, 2014). However, these newfound skills are erratic and inconsistent, as evidenced by the reactive and reflective nature of late adolescence.

BRAIN DEVELOPMENT DURING ADOLESCENCE

Adolescence is an extremely busy time for the brain since this developmental phase involves a tremendous amount of neurological transition. Basically, the adolescent brain is still under construction in that it undergoes dramatic structural changes, with significant reorganization particularly in the region of the prefrontal cortex. This reorganization process involves pruning of neural connections that are not used and growth of other connections, both of which are influenced by adolescents' experiences (Montgomery, 2013). This pruning phenomenon occurs as a critical aspect of early brain development in the first years of life, and again as a secondary wave of pruning during adolescence. This growth and pruning result in an increase in prefrontal cortical integration, which "enables such diverse abilities as cognitive control, emotional regulation, gist thinking, self-understanding and social functions to change and emerge throughout adolescence" (Siegel, 2013, p. 88). On a daily basis, adolescents encounter increased demands on their time and attention as well as thoughts and feelings. Therefore, these gains in brain activity are crucial as adolescents' new life experiences include the multitude of changes that entering and completing high school involves. This includes the challenge of navigating a larger physical and social environment as they enter a world that is more emotionally and cognitively demanding. They are confronted with the need to develop the skill set to track an intensified schedule of course assignments, projects, deadlines, and due dates while balancing them against both school-based and outside of school extracurricular activities. An adolescent's capacity to sense time is an outgrowth of prefrontal cortical integration, which is evidenced as they "begin to dream about the future, wonder about the meaning of life, and to grapple with the reality of death" (Siegel, 2013, p. 232).

Since adolescents' brains are still undergoing development, they can struggle with incorrectly identifying the meaning behind facial expressions, impulsivity, the influence of peers and taking risks, sensitivity to the effects of drugs and alcohol, being enticed by high-excitement and low-effort experiences, and problems with long-term planning (Montgomery, 2013). This helps to explain adolescent behavior that confounds the adults in their lives. Adolescent behavior may not match adults' expectations, which can add to the emotional storminess of this developmental phase. They do not always make the best decisions, and adults are often surprised when their bright, thoughtful, studious, polite, poised, and rule-following adolescent impulsively veers off course.

Given this extremely important period of brain development and the plasticity of the adolescent brain, there are interesting implications for the impact of loss, grief, and trauma. As the prefrontal cortex is adjusting to the growing pains of integration, adolescents struggle with the ability to self-regulate regarding their emotions. This is especially true when confronted with many of the emotions related to loss, grief, and trauma such as fear, sadness, anxiety, guilt, and confusion. The adults in their lives may notice a resultant increase in scanning for danger, or an emotional hypervigilance as adolescents respond to the uncertainty and unpredictability of life. The ways in which adolescents learn or are guided to manage and cope with their loss, grief, and trauma responses will have important neurological and emotional effects that last into adulthood.

CHAPTER 2

The Nature of Adolescent Loss, Grief, and Trauma Responses

Adolescent loss, grief, and trauma responses are distinctly different from those of children, and do not necessarily parallel the loss, grief, and trauma responses of adults (Malone, Garcia, & Pomeroy, 2011). Therefore, both assessment and treatment of adolescents confronting loss, grief, and trauma necessitates approaches that differ from those utilized with children and adults. Notably, adolescent loss, grief, and trauma responses may involve mourning that comes and goes, and the overall process may extend over a long period of time (Hogan & DeSantis, 1996). Adolescent grieving and response to trauma is paradoxically continuous and intermittent (Balk & Corr, 1996). This can be quite confusing to the adolescent's family, friends, and others in his support system. He may isolate and appear sad, and then become more social and seemingly like his old self, and then return to grieving deeply. This can even be confusing and confounding to the adolescent himself. However, it is important to keep in mind that some adolescents are naturally resilient, and have support systems in the form of family, religious or spiritual systems, and caring others that aid them in navigating and coping with loss, grief, and trauma (Malone, 2012).

Adolescents can experience multiple emotions that exist separately, coexist, or alternate (Webb, 2002). Adolescent loss, grief, and trauma responses may include a sense of bravado, denial, anger and rage, shock, numbness, fear of one's own death, nightmares, insomnia, loneliness, survivor guilt, school problems, great sadness, substance abuse, and suicidal ideation (Rheingold, Smith, Ruggiero, Saunders, Kilpatrick, & Resnick, 2004; Ringler & Hayden, 2000). Adolescents are typically reluctant to show strong emotions, making it difficult to assess the nature and depth of their emotional pain. Their natural and expected narcissism can at times make them difficult to reach, particularly when they experience the untimely death of a friend or family member, as well as an unexpected traumatic situation (Goodman, 2002).

Adolescents live intensely in the present and the experience of a death loss causes them to unexpectedly look into the future at the possibility of their own death (Kandt, 1994). This is an unfamiliar concept, since most adolescents do not have as many experiences with loss and death as do adults. An adolescent's sense of safety and security about the world and ongoing relationships may be skewed as a result, particularly in response to the death of a peer (Saltzman, Layne, & Pynoos, 2002). This is especially true given that the majority of peer deaths are sudden, providing no time for preparation for this loss.

Adolescents are often invested in projecting an image of independence and control over their lives, not wanting to need adults. They may delay or repress their grieving in order to keep up this appearance. Adolescents can look like adults in physique, body development, and attire yet still struggle with the emotional immaturity of their age (Noppe & Noppe, 2004). The adults in their lives may react to this pseudosophistication with unrealistic expectations for emotional control. These adolescents may look like they are doing well, but they may in fact be postponing their loss, grief, and trauma reactions, which can reemerge later in adulthood (Kandt, 1994). Typically, adolescents endure an overwhelming sense of being forever changed by their experience of loss, grief, and trauma. This "changed self" does not reflect their previous carefree, invulnerable self, and instead they may appear more fearful and reflective than previously to the loss or trauma event (Lattanzi-Licht, 1996).

The experience of loss, grief, or trauma in adolescence can upset or complicate, but most certainly have an impact on, identity formation, which may already be unstable (O'Brien, Goodenow, & Espin, 1991). Adolescents have not developed the social or emotional maturity to fully incorporate and process loss, grief, and trauma experiences into a coherent worldview (Rowling, 2002). Most adolescents do not possess the frame of reference or context in which to place these profound experiences. Additionally, coping with loss, grief, and trauma is not a typical phase in the life of an adolescent.

Adolescents tend to seek out one another when they have experienced loss, grief, or trauma. If this experience involved the death of a friend or peer, they may feel most comfortable talking with other adolescents who had been close to the deceased. Yet simultaneously, they can feel different from and misunderstood by their peers (Ringler & Hayden, 2000). Adolescents do not typically want to stand out as too very different from their peers, and a loss, grief, or trauma experience may mark them as the person whose father just died, or the kid whose girlfriend died by suicide. Additionally, they may feel discomfort talking with parents about feelings, often disappointed in parents' reactions (O'Brien et al., 1991). Many adolescents expect more support from parents than they actually receive. Parents are unsure how to react to their adolescent, given the image of pseudosophistication and bravado and of not needing parental input. If a peer has died, parents may not understand the depth of their adolescent's grief responses, especially if the deceased peer was not a best friend. An adolescent's perception of lack of parental support makes it difficult for him to find people he can trust with whom to talk about his loss, grief, or trauma experience.

RISK FACTORS

Risk factors are those variables in an adolescent's life that add to the difficulty he may undergo when experiencing loss, grief, and trauma. Risk factors may include the experience of previous losses and traumatic experiences, isolation, few friends or close relationships, problematic relationships with friends or family, substance use and/or abuse, low self-esteem, and poor school performance, which can certainly complicate a current loss, grief, or trauma experience (Balk, 1996; Brown & Gilligan, 1992). Previous losses or traumatic experiences may be triggered, adding a layered effect of sadness, grief, and despair. Adolescents who tend to isolate, who have few friends or close relationships, are at risk for developing an intractable or prolonged grief reaction. With no one to whom he can turn or with whom he can talk, an adolescent is left with his own thoughts and feelings, with little to no ability to gain perspective. The subjective experience of loss, grief, and trauma can be extremely lonely and isolating, adding to or promoting dysfunctional thoughts and behavior. Problematic relationships with friends or family members is another risk factor for adolescents since it makes it difficult for them to turn to these same people for much needed comfort, understanding, and support. Familial risk factors may include the existence of severe emotional turmoil as it relates to a member of the family that has medical, mental health, substance abuse, or anger management problems. Issues of poverty, financial instability, and housing insecurity have an additional impact on an adolescent confronted with loss, grief, and trauma.

Adolescents who use or abuse alcohol or drugs may increase their usage, ultimately numbing or blunting thoughts and feelings of loss, grief, and trauma. Unfortunately, they also numb or blunt more positive emotions that could be beneficial in working through or making meaning of the loss, grief, or trauma experience. Adolescents with low self-esteem are also at risk of not being able to process loss, grief, and trauma, further lessening their view of self. They may feel unlike their peers, that they are somehow branded as different by their loss, grief, or trauma experience, which adds to their already poor view of self. Poor school performance is another potential risk factor in that the loss, grief, or trauma experience may put adolescents even further behind their peers since they may have trouble concentrating or even lose interest in anything related to school or being around other people. This increases their chances of failing classes or even the entire grade, which puts them at greater risk for dropping out of school.

PROTECTIVE FACTORS

Protective factors are those characteristics that help adolescents navigate through loss, grief, and trauma with an intact sense of self. Protective factors may include good relationships with friends and family, a sense of connection to the school community, involvement in extracurricular activities, a healthy level of self-esteem, good school grades, and parental involvement with clear and consistent behavioral boundaries.

Adolescents who have good relationships with friends and family members will have the necessary support through difficult times. They will have people to turn to, depend on, and with whom to walk through the difficulty involved in loss, grief, and trauma. Good relationships often entail a sense of trust as well as a capacity for being understood. In response to a question about who offered support in his grief surrounding his best friend's death by suicide, 17 year-old Tommy stated, "My mom and my dad and my brother. They helped me. They helped by giving me, . . . by encouraging me to go on." Some adolescents are more comfortable grieving with family members than with peers, as evidenced by 14 year-old Kaitlin's loss and grief experience regarding her teacher's sudden death: "No, just my mom. She's the only one I can talk to. And my friends, they were talking among themselves. I felt kind of uncomfortable barging in. Well, let me tell you about me. I felt uncomfortable with them." Adolescents who feel close to their parents and who believe that their parents care about them are able to turn to them during times of loss, grief, and trauma. After experiencing the sudden death of her cousin from a recurrent cancer, 16 year-old Angelica noted, "I have all my friends and family. Me and my mom are best friends. Yeah, she was a big help. She hugged me and said it would be okay."

A sense of connection to the school community is a protective factor since it typically offers an adolescent the opportunity for engagement and connection to friends, peers, teachers, counselors, coaches, and other adults. Adolescents who believe teachers treat them fairly and care about them are able to turn to them for support in response to loss, grief, and trauma. Possessing this positive school bond optimizes the possibility of having more entrusted others that adolescents can have in their circle of support. Similarly, adolescents who are involved in extracurricular activities can be part of a team or group of other adolescents with a shared interest. This creates a place where they can belong and be a part of something outside of their loss, grief, or trauma experience. These activities offer the possibility of being a normal adolescent who laughs, plays, and engages with others. Involvement in these activities creates a healthy respite from the emotions associated with loss, grief, and trauma; a healthy level of self-esteem; good school grades; and parental involvement. Members of the high school band, riding in two different cars, were returning from having dinner prior to the football game when one of the cars became involved in an accident. Two of the adolescent passengers died at the scene. Natalie, an 18 year-old trumpet player, described the support she received: "The whole band was behind my back and it was really good. Yeah, I talked with friends in band. 'Cause EMS, they said he was just sleeping, but I knew he was dead. He just wasn't moving. Yeah, band friends helped."

Adolescents who are part of cohesive friendship groups and social networks that are designed to increase positive connection and personal and collective strengths and competence, and who exhibit high self-esteem, are likely to face loss, grief, and trauma experiences with fewer long-lasting negative effects (Bearman & Moody, 2004; Steese et al., 2006). Strong social bonding is beneficial to adolescents who need support and understanding. After 15 year-old Jack's father was incarcerated, he noted that "Friends were really caring and understood. They supported me." The quality of the connection with others contributes to adolescents' psychological health, self-image, and relationships.

Adolescents who possess the ability to perceive themselves as worthwhile tend to have the capacity for managing or coping with loss, grief, and trauma better than adolescents who have a lesser view of self (Rask, Kaunonen, & Paunonen-Ilmonen, 2002). This is especially important since a significant experience of loss, grief, and trauma changes an adolescent's perspective of himself and his relationship to others. When an adolescent perceives himself as worthwhile, it benefits him in adapting to and coping with the aftermath of a loss, grief, and trauma experience. Adolescents who evidence such individual characteristics as positive coping skills, problem-solving ability, educational achievement, affect regulation, and positive self-esteem possess important tools in managing their loss, grief, and trauma responses.

ADOLESCENT LOSS, GRIEF, AND TRAUMA RESPONSES

Adolescent loss, grief, and trauma responses can be viewed within a developmental framework that includes the physical, social, emotional, and cognitive domains discussed in chapter one. The loss, grief, and trauma responses of adolescents can be placed in these four main domains as physical loss, grief, and trauma responses; social loss, grief, and trauma responses; emotional loss, grief, and trauma responses; and cognitive loss, grief, and trauma responses (see Table 2.1). Each of these domains is described in detail along with quotes from grieving adolescents.

Table 2.1 Adolescent Loss, Grief, and Trauma Responses (Malone, 2007)

Physical	*Social*	*Emotional*	*Cognitive*
Headaches	Feeling different from peers	Dazed	Decline in school performance
Sleep disturbances	Perception of peers being intolerant of their grief	Numb	Paranormal (hallucinatory) experiences
Muscle pain and tension	Social isolation	Shocked	Preoccupation
Stomachaches	Isolation from family	Afraid	Thoughts of own death
Eating disturbances/ Trouble eating	Risk-taking behavior	Frustrated	Sense of presence of the deceased
Joint pain	Increased sense of maturity	Depressed	Realization of the permanency of death
Being ill more often	Experience of unkind remarks from peers	Alone	Disbelief
Lump in throat	Avoidance of reminders	Anxious	Confusion
Tightness in chest	Antisocial	Guilty	Distracted
Aching and heavy arms and legs	Withdrawal from normal activities	Uncomfortable when happy	Difficulty with concentration
Muscle weakness	Change in peer group	Sad	Intrusive thoughts
Dry mouth	Self-destructive behavior	Irritable	Lowered self-esteem
Lack of energy		Vulnerable	Memory problems
Eating disturbances		Angry	
		Aggressive	

Physical Loss, Grief, and Trauma Responses

Research supports a relationship between bodily complaints and physical loss, grief, and trauma responses among adolescents (Servaty & Hayslip, 2001). It may also suggest that adolescents hold loss, grief, and trauma responses in a more physical capacity, unsure of how to express them in physically appropriate ways. In Western society, we are mostly unaware of how loss, grief, and trauma lands in the body, commonly experiencing it as somatic complaints that include headaches, stomachaches, heaviness, muscle tension, a fast heartbeat, a cold sensation, heavy arms and legs, and an overall pressure or a general sense of fatigue. Some adolescents describe immediate physical reactions to learning about a loss, grief, or trauma event whereas others may be too shocked to notice anything at first but then experience a delayed physical reaction. The primary somatic complaint among adolescents is headaches (Malone, 2012). "I had a headache. I know that I had a bad headache. I was just crying. My heart just hurt," said 15 year-old Tameka after learning of a classmate's fatal motorcycle accident. After 14 year-old Malcolm received a phone call from his mother that his younger brother was hit by a car and hospitalized but survived, he stated, "My head was hurting. From the neck down I was numb. My head was hurting."

The next most prevalent somatic complaint by adolescents is difficulty with sleep, being able to fall asleep or stay asleep, with many reporting changes in sleep patterns and issues surrounding sleep in general (Malone, 2012). Many describe struggling with insomnia either because they cannot fall asleep or they do not want to let go enough to fall sleep. Latoya, a 15 year-old whose deceased grandmother raised her, states, "I kept on waking up in the middle of the night and not being able to go to sleep again. Sometimes I still wake up. I wonder if she's watching me." The fear of nightmares or of dreaming about the loss, grief, or trauma event can keep some adolescents from sleeping. As noted by 18 year-old Benjamin, who witnessed a fatal car accident, "I would wake up with nightmares. I kept replaying the scene of the car flipped over and people being carried away." Many adolescents describe having vivid dreams that involve their deceased loved one, which creates a longing and desire to see them again or to sleep and dream about them. One adolescent girl noted that she often cried in her sleep and was awoken by her alarmed mother. "I was crying in my sleep. My mom would run into my room," states 13 year-old Linda, whose younger brother died of leukemia. Other sleep issues may include insomnia, mid-cycle waking with the inability to fall back to sleep, and taking a long time to initially fall asleep. "I keep waking up at 1 or 2 in the morning. I go to sleep but then I wake up. I try to find something on TV. I think about how he died. And then I think my brother's gonna die," declares 15 year-old Marina, whose friend died by gang violence, and whose brother is a gang member. After 16 year-old Jason witnessed a band member die in a car accident, he describes his inability to sleep for weeks: "I felt really tired and then I couldn't sleep. My mom was like 'I don't know what to do for you. Maybe take you to the doctor's 'cause you're not sleeping at all.' I was just thinking and thinking and I couldn't go to sleep." Sleep issues seem to be related to thinking about the event. As stated by 15 year-old Marinda after her brother was killed by rival gang members, "I overthink and I get really bad headaches and I cannot go to sleep because I'm thinking everything even if I don't want to think about it. It takes control of me. My anger takes control of me." More sleep issues are described by 17 year-old Stacey after hearing about the murder of a friend. "I was tired, all over my body. I was just worn out. I felt like I had been running like for days, just worn out. And then I couldn't sleep and I wanted to sleep and I was afraid." Some adolescents describe trying to distract themselves to keep from sleeping for fear of dreaming. They typically find themselves stuck in a thinking loop about the loss, grief, or trauma event or about other worries and concerns, which can deter them from attempting sleep. As noted by 16 year-old Marcus, whose parents died in a flood, "I would go for days without sleeping. I would just stay awake, play with my dogs, eat, play games on my Xbox, just anything to keep myself occupied because I knew I would start dreaming. And when I'd start dreaming, and that's when it started to hurt because I'd remember, and then you start hoping and wishing it's not true." Another adolescent reports only being able to sleep with the lights on, and another only if someone is awake in the house. These descriptions of sleep issues suggest that the act of letting go toward an unconscious state is both difficult and frightening. Daily routines, particularly sleep cycles, can be impacted and changed by the experience of loss, grief, or trauma.

Eating can become an issue for adolescents impacted by loss, grief, and trauma. Appetites can range from having no appetite at all, with a complete inability to eat, to some adolescents being absolutely ravenous, with the inability to stop eating. These two extremes can last for various periods, from a day to weeks to months at a time. Some adolescents may describe that their appetites are forever changed, noting that food no longer tastes right or good following a loss, grief, or trauma event. As noted by 13 year-old Tom, whose dog was run over by a car, "I couldn't eat for about two weeks. I couldn't eat. Food didn't taste good." Some adolescents may experience a nausea reaction to food. This is described by 14 year-old Jackie, whose father was incarcerated for theft. "There were periods when I didn't want to eat at all. Like I just didn't want to eat. I was just so upset and angry and so nauseous." Others may lose their appetite for periods of time, leading to weight loss. One adolescent girl continued to lose weight due to the experience of multiple deaths and traumas, to the point that her physician expressed concern. Once a lost appetite returns, however, some adolescents may describe being unable to stop eating, continuously grazing, which results in unwanted weight gain. As noted by 16 year-old Jason, whose twin sister died in a scuba diving accident, "I didn't eat. Physically I knew I had to eat. Now I eat everything. I can't stop eating. It's nonstop. I'm always hungry." Tanisha, an 18 year-old who was cheated on by her boyfriend of three years, said, "I would go days without eating. Then I ate a lot and gained weight."

The entire body can be affected by loss, grief, and trauma experiences. Delaney, a 14 year-old whose parents divorced, said, "My body felt dead. I was always tired and always wanted to sleep. And I wasn't sleeping and I just kept exercising. My body was just tired. It was tired and it felt sick." Some adolescents feel the need to push their bodies to manage the impact of loss, grief, and trauma. As described by 17 year-old Taylor, whose father died of an aneurysm, "And then I lost a lot of weight. The doctor said I had to gain more weight. I had very low body fat. I wasn't trying to lose weight. I was in marching band and that keeps you moving. I was eating. I was just, when there was a lull in one of my classes, I would do pushups, like wall pushups, just to have something to do. And then sometimes I would run in the morning before my classes. I guess I was nervous. I was drained, completely drained." As 16 year-old Jolene expressed when she received a text message about her aunt's death, "I was really tense at first. But then afterward when I was with my boyfriend, I couldn't hold anything back. I lost all control. My muscles weren't tense. If I had fallen myself on the ground, I wouldn't have been able to get back up because I was so heartbroken." The physical or somatic response to loss, grief, and trauma can be sudden and intense. Lila, a 15 year-old whose friend was murdered, describes her reaction as "Like there was some pain. Like my stomach was cramping. Head was hurtin'. My arms felt like there was something on them and I couldn't lift them up. And my legs were like they were taped to the chair so I couldn't get up. It was hard. It hurt." Adolescents can recognize a physical feeling akin to being in shock. "My body felt hurt and broken. Felt like everything was broken.

Table 2.2   Physical Loss, Grief, and Trauma Response Themes

My body hurts	*Eating is a problem*	*I can't sleep*
Headaches	No appetite	Insomnia
Muscle tension	• lost weight	Nightmares
Fatigue	• food tastes different	Crying in sleep
Fast heartbeat	• for weeks	Mid-cycle waking
Cold sensation	Ravenous	Long time to fall asleep
Heavy arms and legs	• cannot stop eating	Sleeping with lights on
Pressure	• hungry all the time	Sleeping when someone is awake
	• gained weight	
	Food does not taste good	

I was in shock. I had this cold sensation. It was like this pressure," is the response from 16 year-old Josh, whose younger sister died by suicide. Other adolescents describe their reaction to loss, grief, and trauma as "Really, really weak and angry," "I hurt all over," and "I mean sadness takes over my body and then everything hurts. I don't sleep, I don't eat." Table 2.2 captures the physical loss, grief, and trauma response themes described by these adolescents.

Social Loss, Grief, and Trauma Responses

Social loss, grief, and trauma responses provide information about an adolescent's social world to include with whom she feels comfortable talking and who belongs to her support system. It is important to gain information about her family and friends' reactions to her loss, grief, and trauma experience. The ways in which caring others approach and respond to a grieving adolescent can have an impact on how she copes with loss, grief, and trauma. If she receives negative or hurtful comments or statements, this may drive her to spend more time alone or to behave in self-destructive ways. Equally important is to learn about how an adolescent spends her time when alone. She may want to stay in her bedroom and not talk to anyone, with the desire to stay away from all reminders of her loss, grief, and trauma experience. Yet, other adolescents state that their attempts to not talk about their loss, grief, or trauma experience resulted in their feeling even more alone.

The majority of adolescents affirm they have people they turn to who understand what they need, who are supportive and caring. These typically include an adolescent's parents, older brothers and sisters, boyfriends or girlfriends, friends, and sometimes teachers as their support system. As described by Alicia, a 17 year-old whose classmate died in a car accident, "I talk to my dad and my boyfriend a lot. I have always gotten along with guys. I've never been a girly girl. I talk to my dad a lot and he was more upset about it than I was because he just can't stand losing somebody younger than him." As stated by 13 year-old Tom, whose dog was run over by a car, "I talk to my mom and my dad. Sometimes my brother. But I don't want comfort. I just want to cry." Siblings can be very helpful, as described by 17 year-old Stacey, whose friend was murdered, "My older brother who's in college. I can talk to him about anything and everything. He really helps me. He comes to visit." Although some adolescents report feeling understood and supported by parents, others do not. They express disappointment in their parents' reactions, which corresponds with previous studies (O'Brien et al., 1991). This could mean that parents may not recognize the severity of the loss to their adolescent, particularly if the loss is not a death loss or if parents did not perceive their adolescent as very close to the deceased. Tanisha, an 18 year-old who was cheated on by her boyfriend of three years, notes that her mom is not supportive: "She told me to get over it, that I'm young, and there will be plenty of guys. She just does not get it."

Many adolescents state that they feel more grown up than their friends, that they have experienced something often beyond the scope of their peers. This is supported by studies that claim adolescents can feel different from and misunderstood by their peers (Ringler & Hayden, 2000). The reactions of friends can range from "helpful to heartless," with great variance. Some adolescents described friends as being supportive and helpful in that they can cry together, hold one another, go for walks together, and that these friends allow for expression of a range of emotions. "Friends are really caring and understand. They support me." As validated by 16 year-old Benita, whose police officer uncle died in the line of duty, "My friends went wild. They were getting out of class and I told them what happened. We just walked around and cried." Others report that friends are "heartless" in that they blame the deceased for his or her death or joke about it. This is especially true if a death is perceived as avoidable. As described by 15 year-old Marinda after her older brother was killed by rival gang members, "Some of my friends take it as a joke. They say, oh I feel sorry for you, but then at the end they be like, oh you know he asked for it." As told by 17 year-old Stacey, whose friend was murdered, and after their high school principal informed the school community, "I thought they were heartless. It's weird to see other people not react like I do. I was raised to view things differently. I understand now but when that happened I thought everyone should be crying their eyes out." Yet some adolescents describe how very alone they feel, and that there is absolutely no one from whom they could or would seek support. This may have to do with the type of loss, grief, or trauma experience an adolescent endures. For example, 16 year-old Josh, whose younger sister died by suicide, states, "I try not to talk to anybody about it."

The impact of loss, grief, and trauma can cause an adolescent to avoid friendship for fear of losing other people. As noted by Lila, a 15 year-old whose friend was murdered, "Right now, well she was like my sister. It's sometimes kind of hard for me to trust someone. I think that if I trust that friend they might go away." As described by 17 year-old Carissa, who lived through a hurricane that took the lives of her grandfather, cousin, neighbor, and two pet dogs, as well as the loss of the family home and possessions, and who had to relocate to a new state and high school, "I never actually told my friends because of all the people I've lost, it's kind of a bad thing. I've kind of distanced myself from people where I won't have that best friend, or won't have as close friends so when they did die. . . ."

A preference for solitude may also be evidenced by some adolescents, perhaps a change from their norm prior to their loss, grief, or trauma experience, or this may have been typical for that particular adolescent. This tendency toward solitude may indicate that many adolescents gain a sense of peace and calm when alone. As expressed by 17 year-old Thomas, "I was like mad and lonely, but I really wanted to be alone." Needing time alone is a theme that emerges and holds importance when speaking with adolescents who have endured a loss, grief, or trauma experience. They describe this as a necessity. It is interesting to note how adolescents fill this alone time. As described by 15 year-old Martin, who witnessed fellow band members involved in a fatal car accident, "After that I just sat in my room and just watched TV but I didn't really pay attention to what was on. I just sat there. I was thinking in my head like a movie, like it all happened and why. I just wanted to know why. And I like to be alone for this. Now, I watch TV or write in my journal. I like to write how I feel. It helps a lot." Reading books was the way one adolescent boy spent all of his time alone. As expressed by 16 year-old Jason, whose twin sister died in a scuba diving accident, "I read. I create my own world. I really love

Table 2.3   Social Loss, Grief, and Trauma Response Themes

Who supports me	Helpful and heartless friends	I need time alone
Parents	Blaming	Listen to meaningful music
Older siblings	Joking	Read to "create own world"
Friends	Heartless	Escape into computer
No one	Supportive	Want to be alone in room
Self	Cry together	Write/journal about feelings
	Hold one another	

to read. As much as I can. A lot." Some adolescents escape into the computer by spending time on Facebook or playing interactive video games as a way to connect to other adolescents in an environment that they can control. As noted by 17 year-old Thomas, whose football coach died suddenly, "Time alone. It's . . . to be honest with you I'm on the computer, on Facebook, or playing video games. I'm not trying to say it's like my getaway but it's something to spend time." Preference for time alone is expressed by 15 year-old Jack after his father was incarcerated: "Most of the time I go walking and my mom thinks it's weird, that something might happen to me. I want to be alone. I don't want people around me." Overall, it appears that the intention of time alone for adolescents is to maximize control of stimuli and interaction with others. Table 2.3 captures the social loss, grief, and trauma response themes described by adolescents.

Emotional Loss, Grief, and Trauma Responses
Emotional grief and trauma responses in adolescents include an array of feelings that might or might not be displayed. These include feeling dazed, numb, in shock, anxious, guilty, depressed, frustrated, sad, irritable, and angry. By no means is this an exhaustive list of adolescent emotions. The people in grieving and traumatized adolescents' lives often describe a changed or altered adolescent. As noted earlier, adolescents may experience a confusing multitude of emotions. They have yet to develop proficiency in either identifying or regulating their emotions and therefore may enact a fight, flight, or freeze reaction. Adults may experience their grieving adolescent as angry, argumentative, belligerent, or just plain grouchy. This is known as a fight reaction. Another adolescent may isolate by holing up in his room, spending time gaming, reading, or listening to music. This is known as a flight reaction. Yet another adolescent

may seem overwhelmed, unmotivated or lethargic, seemingly unable or unwilling to function as she did previously. This is evidence of a freeze reaction. Without the ability to recognize or label what they are feeling, it can be very difficult for adolescents to ask for help from caring adults. It can also be daunting for adults to determine how to approach or react to their grieving adolescent when they may be experiencing their own loss, grief, and trauma responses. As the mother of a 14 year-old boy whose uncle died stated, "He was always so outgoing. Now he only wants to spend time alone in his room. I worry about him. He doesn't laugh anymore." Some adolescents are stymied or confused about how to react, particularly whether to cry or not to cry. Alicia, a 17 year-old whose classmate died in a car accident, states, "I didn't know how to feel or what to do or what to say." Annamarie, a 16 year-old, heard about her friend's mother's death: "Am I supposed to cry?"

Crying can have different meanings for adolescents (Malone, 2012). Many describe differences about where, when, and with whom they cry. Some cry alone in private, some with family and friends. A couple of adolescents mention not knowing if they are allowed to cry. This seems particularly true if they have had no model for crying in their families. Many boys receive overt and sometimes covert messages about the unmasculine nature of showing tears. This can also be true of girls. Adolescents often hide or camouflage these feelings from adults and from one another (McNeil, Silliman, & Swihart, 1991), especially when uncertain about what to feel and how to express those feelings. The ability to cry may be very easy for some yet very difficult for others. Some adolescents continue to cry and struggle with how to control the urge to cry that can "come out of nowhere." As Jeffrey, a 15 year-old who found out on Facebook about his cousin's death due to a motorcycle accident, states, "I don't know. I was sort of crying on the inside." As continued by Annamarie, a 16 year-old who had learned about her friend's mother's death, "I was like, when I first read the message, am I supposed to cry or what? 'Cause I didn't really feel anything and then whenever I went to go to talk to one of my teachers, like that was when I started breaking down. It was kind of hard for me to breathe, to catch my breath. I just started crying and he was just like I know that you want to throw stuff around and just don't talk to anybody because he's been through that. I was just sitting there crying like loud." When 16 year-old Jolene received a text message about her aunt's death, "I started crying right there in the classroom. And then when I got home I went up to my room and cried some more. I just had to let it out." As noted by 17 year-old Carissa, who experienced multiple losses, grief, and trauma during a hurricane that took the lives of her grandfather, cousin, neighbor, and two pet dogs as well as resulting in the loss of the family home and possessions, "Like I cry sometimes but just like I know when I cry it doesn't get better. I try to be happy. I can so easily be sad." Latoya, a 15 year-old, after the death of the grandmother who raised her, states, "At first I couldn't cry and later that night I just fell apart. I was talking to my boyfriend and he was trying to tell me it's okay, everything's gonna be alright, I'm here, something like that. I was trying to maintain but I just fell apart. I cried then forever."

Some adolescents describe feeling angry. Joseph, a 16 year-old, describes his emotional reaction to hearing about his older brother's death by gang violence: "Because immediately I wanted to go crazy. I had like an intense rage because I was so angry but I couldn't show that in front of my family." Joseph's explanation also underscores the fact that many adolescents are loath to show intense emotions to others, especially family members if these adolescents believe they need to protect the family from such displays of emotion. Sometimes a sense of regret can accompany anger. As 15 year-old Martin, who witnessed fellow band members involved in a fatal car accident, states, "I get mad. I hurt. I feel that now. When I feel happy I then think about them. I wish I had spent more time with them." Descriptions of feeling "good and bad" or "up and down" are common, suggesting that many adolescents maintain awareness of the range of emotions they are capable of experiencing. As described by 16 year-old Benita, whose police officer uncle died in the line of duty, "I don't cry. I'm up and down. One day I'm like so happy and like the next I'm mad at everything. Don't breathe my air. Don't look at me. Don't flip your hair. Everything drives me crazy. And the next day I can't stop crying and I'm crying and I'm crying and I'm crying and I don't know why." Some adolescents express confusion about the array of emotions they can feel in response to loss, grief, and trauma. When 17 year-old Thomas was asked to describe his reaction to hearing about the sudden death of his football coach, he said, "I was really really nervous and just like, I can't really describe how I felt. It took a long time for me to start getting emotional. I just shut down. I was really choked up."

Many adolescents who experience loss, grief, and trauma express concerns about their own death. Adolescents live intensely in the present, and the experience of loss, grief, and trauma causes them to look into the future at the possibility of their own death (Kandt, 1994). This is typically an unfamiliar concept for adolescents. They may also express fear of the next death. Who will it be? Who's next? How and when?

Table 2.4 Emotional Loss, Grief, and Trauma Response Themes

Feelings now	*I worry*
Continues to cry	About own death
The deceased is not coming back	About next death
Good and bad	About friends and family
Up and down	
Enjoyment of life	
Anger and hurt	

Adolescents who experience more than one death loss learn to expect the next one. There is also great concern about friends and family members. Additionally, adolescents who have never experienced a friend or family member's death may become convinced that they will have that experience soon. Adolescents who have experienced prior deaths also have the same worry. These expressions of concerns and worries indicate a sense of being forever changed. This "changed self" does not reflect their previous carefree, invulnerable self and instead is more fearful and reflective (Lattanzi-Licht, 1996). As noted by 17 year-old Carissa, who experienced multiple losses, grief, and trauma during a hurricane that took the lives of her grandfather, cousin, neighbor, and two pet dogs as well as resulting in the loss of the family home and possessions, "[I was] stressed out and then I felt there was a point I wanted to give up on everything. Everything. I didn't feel that there was a point to living. It really really put me in a dark side. Made me think about things and that it was me against the world and everyone's wrong and I'm the only one with all this going on even though I know I'm not." A couple of adolescents who experienced losing loved ones to gang violence explain, "Emotionally things are hard. I care too much and it feels like no one else cares so why should I care. I try not to think about it. Sometimes that works." Table 2.4 captures what Carissa and other adolescents indicate about their emotional responses to loss, grief, and trauma.

Cognitive Loss, Grief, and Trauma Responses
Typically, adolescents have not developed the social or emotional maturity to fully incorporate and process bereavement into a coherent worldview (Rowling, 2002). This explains why many adolescents garner thoughts about the unfairness of loss, grief, and trauma experiences. With little life experience, they may perceive this as being the worst thing

that ever happened to them. This can be especially true if the loss, grief, and trauma experience involves an untimely or unexpected death. Many adolescents view death loss as unfair, especially if it is an untimely death. Although adolescents assume they will outlive their parents, they are rarely prepared to do so at such an early age.

Exploring an adolescent's thoughts, ideas, and beliefs offers important information about how she thinks about her experiences with loss, grief, and trauma, and what meaning she might attach to these experiences. Some adolescents express thoughts about God. As noted by 17 year-old Taylor, whose father died of an aneurysm, "I know that he passed. I just feel like God has him. I don't think so much about his death per se, but just about him." As stated by 15 year-old Marinda after her brother was killed by rival gang members, "Why did he die? Why now? How come God made him come to Him now? My brother says it is because God decided his life would be better in heaven because it was bad here. So he's better off. I believe that. But why am I still here?" One adolescent girl wonders, "Just like where she's at. Like if she is in heaven. Is she up there?" Some adolescents express an acceptance of death, typically in the form of it being that person's time for death, life as being different now, and that they have gained a new perspective and appreciation for their lives from their loss, grief, and trauma experience. As expressed by 13 year-old Linda, whose younger brother died of leukemia, "I think he gave me a better outlook on life. I appreciate my gift of life. Overall, it has just helped me." As expressed by Alicia, a 17 year-old whose classmate died in a car accident, "I guess it was his time to die. I don't understand it. I guess his dying was to show us that there is a reality that we too can die. Anything can happen. Before he died I thought, oh I'm young and I have a lot of life before I die. Now I don't know. . . . All that he showed me, how to be, how to react. I got more mature. I put all those little girl things aside. I just try to have fun with my life but to do things right." As stated by 17 year-old Stacey, whose friend was murdered, "Now I just kind of accept the fact that she's in a better place and that what happened before happened and I should move on. She's supposed to be here with us graduating and going to the prom." As noted by Joseph, a 16 year-old whose older brother died by gang violence, "People leave you at certain times. Life is life and it happens." This perspective can lead adolescents to try to intentionally enjoy life more, and to spend more time with friends and family members.

After a loss, grief, or trauma experience, adolescents can worry and wonder about what might happen next. Marina, a 15 year-old who moved to the United States from Mexico with her family two years ago, and whose friend died by gang violence, also worries about her brother who is a gang member. She states, "Who else is next? We came here and thought it would be better. And people just keep dying." As 18 year-old Benjamin, who witnessed a fatal car accident, attests, he worries about "Just about who's next? I can't take any more death." Lila, a 15 year-old whose friend was murdered, exclaims, "I'm worried about my friends more now. Like, where are you going, what time are you going to check in?!" One adolescent ponders his own death after his parents died in a flood; stated by 16 year-old Marcus, "I'm not worried necessarily about dying but about when or why or how."

Concentration can become a huge problem for many adolescents. Concentration can decrease dramatically following a loss, grief, or trauma experience, and for some, never quite improve. Memory problems can become an issue, with many adolescents noting a drop in grades and with some adolescents failing classes or even the school year.

In discussing what her concentration has been like following her police officer uncle's death in the line of duty, 16 year-old Benita states, "Oh that definitely decreased. At the beginning of school . . . I can't tell you what the teachers said. I don't really know. I've had a hard time concentrating. I think about what my family's doing, are they okay, are they driving, are they on a plane, are they doing okay?" Grades, mentioned by 15 year-old Martin, who witnessed fellow band members involved in a fatal car accident, are "Bad. I can't remember anything. It's like I black out. I'm gone. I go off somewhere." Regarding the school year and concentration, as noted by 16 year-old Marcus, whose parents died in a flood, "Hmmm, not so good. It's like I can't. You know how you pick rocks up? I feel like something has to pull me up out of this hole but it seems like I can't crawl up out of it." After his father was incarcerated, 15 year-old Jack states, "I try but it's really bad. I'm barely passing. I don't feel like doing homework. My mind goes off in other directions."

Some adolescents are able to regain an improved level of concentration to better their grades. "My grades dropped for about 3 weeks or so. Then I was able to focus." One adolescent girl noted successfully making herself focus and burying herself in her schoolwork as a diversion from thinking about her brother's death; her grades were excellent but she described not being able to focus on anything outside of school. Overall, concentration can be a real concern for adolescents experiencing loss, grief, or trauma. Table 2.5 captures what adolescents have to say about the impact of loss, grief, and trauma on their cognitive abilities.

Table 2.5 Cognitive Loss, Grief, and Trauma Response Themes

She's/he's dead	I can't concentrate
Unfairness	Decreased ability to focus
Time for his/her death	Memory problems
More acceptance	Go off somewhere
Angry at God	Grades drop
Worst thing that ever happened	
Life is different now	
New perspective	

DISENFRANCHISED GRIEF

The disenfranchised nature of adolescent grief is a phenomenon "that is shaped fundamentally by the grieving rules of parents, other adults, and peers, all of whom create the grieving norms of an adolescent's world" (Rowling, 2002, p. 276). Adolescents are often perceived as resilient and not seriously affected by loss and grief (Ringler & Hayden, 2000). Adults may not recognize the severity of the loss, grief, or trauma event to an adolescent. Disenfranchisement occurs when an adolescent's grief is inhibited by established "grieving norms that deny grief to persons deemed to have insignificant losses, insignificant relationships, or an insignificant capacity to grieve" (Doka, 2002, p. xiii). Types of loss that may be categorized as disenfranchised include those where the relationship with the deceased is not recognized, the loss is not acknowledged, and there is exclusion of the griever (Doka, 2002). In many instances, this encompasses the experience that adolescents face when a classmate or friend dies. The death of an adolescent's peer or classmate is often an unrecognized loss by others. This death loss may be viewed by parents, teachers, and friends as unimportant in an adolescent's life, especially if the peer or classmate was not someone the adolescent hung out with or appeared very close to. This also relates to the death of a peer who had been a former friend where there was limited current contact (Doka, 2002). The deceased may have been an adolescent's ex-boyfriend or ex-girlfriend. An added layer of complexity can complicate loss if the relationship between the deceased and an adolescent had been an unrecognized, unsupported, or otherwise not sanctioned gay or lesbian relationship. This creates a hidden population of secret survivors, experiencing disenfranchised grief. Adolescent grief often goes unnoticed, is apt to be minimized by others, or is misunderstood (Sklar & Hartley, 1990). Adding to the impact of loss is the suddenness that typically characterizes adolescent deaths.

Adolescents may be excluded and omitted from funerals and memorials of a deceased peer or classmate because they are not family members. This is also true for ex-boyfriends or ex-girlfriends. There appear to be grieving rules that "limit grief to the deaths of family members," thereby disallowing, or "disenfranchising," an adolescent's grief in response to the death of a peer (Doka, 2002, p. 6). Adolescents have few rights as mourners (Sklar, 1991), are at times viewed as not having the capacity to grieve, and are typically advised to focus on their schoolwork and other relationships.

CHAPTER 3

Non-Death Loss in the Lives of Adolescents

This chapter explores non-death loss in the lives of adolescents and the impact this has on adolescents. There is a long list of possible non-death losses that may occur in the lives of adolescents (see Table 3.1). Some of these non-death losses are secondary losses that occur after a death loss. For example, the death of a parent may be followed by a change in finances, which could lead to relocation, a change in school, and, therefore, change in or loss of the previous friendship group. Relocation could be due to a change in parental employment or parental military service reassignment. Both primary and secondary losses may be due to survival

Table 3.1   Non-Death Loss During Adolescence

Non-Death Loss
Parental separation/divorce
Incarceration of a parent
Parental military deployment
Relocation due to financial change
Relocation due to military reassignment
Relocation due to change in employment
Relocation due to natural disaster
Material/neighborhood loss due to natural disaster
Friendship loss
Romantic breakup
Change of school
Loss of physical safety
Loss of innocence
Loss of childhood

of a natural disaster. Many trauma experiences during adolescence may involve loss of physical safety, as in the case of natural disasters and from growing up in a violent neighborhood or household; loss of innocence, as in the case of rape or attempted homicide; and loss of childhood, as in the case of parental death that results in an adolescent becoming parentified. The non-death losses explored in this chapter include parental divorce, incarceration of a parent, some of the many reasons for relocation, friendship loss, and romantic breakup.

PARENTAL DIVORCE
Each year more than 1 million children and adolescents in the United States experience the divorce of their parents, and 21 million children and adolescents currently live with just one parent (U.S. Bureau of the Census, 2012). Consider the impact when more than half of all divorces in the United States involve children and adolescents, and the alarming fact that about 40% of adolescents experience the divorce of their parents (Amato, 2000). Although many children and adolescents survive the impact of their parents' divorce with resilience and good coping skills and develop into well-adjusted individuals (Kelly, 2007), there are many who do not. Parental divorce during the adolescent years is correlated with an array of symptoms to include poor school grades, difficulty with peer relationships, behavioral acting out, psychosomatic complaints, angst, anger, sadness, feeling unloved, physical and emotional distancing, and an increase in internalizing problems (Amato & Anthony, 2014; Wallerstein & Lewis, 2004). Prior to the divorce, the family may have experienced conflict, chaos, and some amount of disorganization, which may or may not improve following the divorce. However, some adolescents notice little to no overt conflict between their parents (Amato & Hohmann-Marriott, 2007), which can make parental divorce an unexpected and surprising loss to an adolescent.

Divorce presents challenges and risks, and is an emotionally complex situation for families that creates multiple transitions, both beneficial and detrimental. Some of these transitions may include a change in residence, bouncing back and forth between two different households, a change in school and friendship groups, an impact on finances, and a shift in parent-adolescent relationships. Divorce changes many things in an adolescent's life such as where he may live, his relationship with each parent, exposure to adult/parental conflict, and the standard of living he was accustomed to (Amato & Anthony, 2014). An added stressor is that many parents "remarry or recouple within 5 years of their divorce" (Ahrons, 2007, p. 56). A parental remarriage or recoupling may bring stepsiblings, which impacts the parent-adolescent relationship. For example, an adolescent who is an only child may now have to share her parent not only with another adult but with other children, as is also the case should the new couple have a child between them. She may also struggle with a parent who has not remarried or recoupled and is unhappy with the other parent's new relationship status. If both parents remarry or recouple, she then has more people with which to negotiate how to live together. This can have an impact on the developmental task of identity formation at a time when an adolescent is learning about who she is and what is important to her. She needs her parents but may be hesitant to rely on them as they themselves are navigating their new relationship status.

Reactions to separation and divorce may vary among adolescents depending on the specific circumstances. The severity and duration of negative responses is also dependent on the presence of a variety of protective and risk factors (Amato, 2000). These factors involve the quality and nature of the relationship between adolescent and each parent, the degree of her involvement in the school community, whether or not she has a dependable friend and peer support group, her grades in school, and her own well-being and mental health, particularly if she struggles with depression and/or anxiety. Adolescents enduring parental divorce may experience phases of grieving similar to those associated with death and dying (Shulman, 2005). Divorce represents the termination of the family unit and is often characterized as a painful loss to many adolescents. Similar to the death of a parent, divorce impacts adolescents by putting them at higher risk for a number of affective disorders and mental health problems, both during adolescence and into adulthood (Luecken & Appelhans, 2005). It impacts adolescents' ability to trust and rely on the adults in their lives. The period during a divorce may involve tremendous emotional distress, confusion, relationship strain, and life upheaval for both adolescents and their parents (Emery & Forehand, 1996). This is dependent on the nature of the parental relationship prior to the divorce, and the ways in which adolescents are informed about the impending divorce. Some parents over-share with their adolescent by divulging information that is adult in nature and should stay between the adults. Others place blame and attempt to have the adolescent choose sides. Some parents give no reasonable or understandable explanation, leaving adolescents to guess about the reasons for the divorce, often finding themselves as the cause for the family split. Divorce involves loss of attachment to parents and the revision of a life plan that an adolescent has come to expect and depend on (Bernstein, 2006). They are now products of a divorced family and assume many of the negative stereotypes that go along with being a child of divorce. Adolescents may perceive their parents' divorce as "unexpected, unwelcome, and unpredictable" (Booth & Amato, 2001). That which was familiar transforms into an unknown and uncertain future. Divorce can have lingering, subtle effects that shadow adolescence.

Adolescents are often thrust into premature autonomy as they attempt to deal with negative feelings about the divorce and their de-idealization of each parent (Cohen, 2002). Their anger, confusion, and sense of betrayal combined with the challenge of adolescent development makes dealing with parental divorce quite daunting. Younger adolescents, ages 13 to 14, may immerse themselves in activities to distract themselves from their emotions (Malone, 2011). These younger adolescents are often characterized by an avoidance of all emotional expression, particularly any public display of their feelings (Christ, 2000). They are unsure how to feel in response to a situation over which they have no control as well as no involvement in the decision. They tend to focus on activities where they can exert more control. Older adolescents, ages 15 to 18, describe intense emotions that interfere with enjoying their normal routines, including school and involvement in extracurricular activities (Christ, 2000). Some adolescents opt out of their involvement in extracurricular activities due to change in financial status or self-imposed caretaking of an emotionally overwhelmed parent or younger siblings. They may also experience a decrease in their former level of energy or desire to remain involved in these activities. In response to their parents' divorce, adolescents often feel different from their peers, experience self-blame, and have a heightened sensitivity to interpersonal relationships (Davies & Cummings, 1994). If most of his friends have intact families, his parents' divorce may cause him to stand out from other adolescents, which is an experience that most adolescents loathe. They do not want to be spotlighted for fear of being judged, ridiculed, or stigmatized. They may exhibit behavior such as substance use or abuse, poor school performance, somatic complaints, inappropriate sexual behavior, depression, anxiety, aggressive behavior, and delinquent behavior as a response to complex emotions caused by their parents' divorce (Clarke-Stewart et al., 2000).

Many adolescents refuse to risk the trust and vulnerability involved in being close to someone again (Malone, 2011). They tend to remain vigilant to other possible losses, particularly in regard to relationships, choosing to not get close to friends or other family members. They remain vulnerable to affective disorders such as anxiety and depression, especially during times of high life stress (Luecken & Appelhans, 2005). The years during high school present many situations that can create a high level of stress for adolescents, such as the focus on achieving good grades, the entire application process for those seeking to attend college, and the intricacies of developing and maintaining relationships with people both within and outside of the school community. Further complicating this is that adolescents may embrace the concept of having a damaged identity due to being the child of divorce, dismiss parental efforts to help alleviate their stress, isolate themselves from the family, and develop symptoms that act as reminders that parents have hurt them (Bernstein, 2006). They may not be ready to relinquish their feelings of anger, distrust, and hurt (Malone, 2011). Not having the emotional bandwidth to manage this myriad of feelings, adolescents will either externalize these feelings by acting out or internalize them by developing anxiety, depression, or a very low view of self.

INCARCERATION OF A PARENT

The United States has the highest incarceration rate and recidivism rate as compared to other countries (Nichols & Loper, 2012). It is imperative to consider both the short-term and long-terms effects this has on adolescents who lose a parent to prison. Given the separation individuation process inherent in and a crucial component of healthy adolescent development, incarceration of a parent disrupts an adolescent's attachment to an important adult in the adolescent's life. The separation of an adolescent from his or her parent due to incarceration impairs that attachment. The timing of this occurs just when an adolescent is striving for independence and must have a secure base or attachment from which to separate in healthy and meaningful ways. This forced separation can lead to feelings of abandonment and environmental instability, and it alters their belief about the world being a safe, predictable, and just place. An insecure attachment relationship to an incarcerated parent is correlated with adolescent substance use and abuse and with delinquent or acting out behavior (Midgley & Lo, 2013). The loss, grief, and trauma associated with the parent's arrest, trial, and subsequent incarceration can create complexities in what is already an adjustment to the adolescent years.

The remaining parent may be less responsive and available to the adolescent, which can have an impact on their relationship, leaving the adolescent to feel even more alone. Many of the effects of parental incarceration can be similar to or mimic those of parental divorce and parental death. Adolescents may take on a parentified role in the family toward younger siblings as well as a more adult and emotionally caretaking role toward the remaining parent. This is beyond the scope of responsibility that an adolescent should take on, yet this does occur in many family situations that involve parental incarceration. Adolescents may lack an opportunity within the family to discuss their experience of having an incarcerated parent, and they may hide or camouflage their feelings and thoughts in order to maintain some peace and calm in an otherwise disrupted household. The result of an adolescent keeping emotionally quiet is that it adds to her feelings of loneliness and differentness. Adolescents may experience a sense of stigmatization, which is associated with feelings of shame and guilt in response to a real or perceived rejection by the school community, neighborhood, and peers (Nichols & Loper, 2012). Adolescents of an incarcerated parent are more likely to experience emotional disorders, behavioral issues, adjustment problems, involvement in criminal behavior and aggressive delinquent acts, lower self-esteem, and substance use and abuse (Crawford, 2003; Midgley & Lo, 2013; Phillips, Burns, Wagner, Kramer, & Robbins, 2002). Many adolescents with incarcerated parents may have endured years of trauma-inducing situations to include exposure to violence, a heightened sense of vigilance, instability in living environment and finances, and a continuous insecurity. This has an impact on the developing adolescent identity regarding who she is becoming as an early adolescent, late adolescent, and eventually emerging adult who has had to make decisions about who to turn to for support, understanding, and guidance. Many learn to trust no one due to the unreliability, upheaval, disorganization, and multifaceted life disruption of the family environment.

Research on the ways in which adolescents navigate the stressors that accompany parental incarceration suggests that adolescents use a combination of three specific strategies: deidentification from their incarcerated parent, desensitization to the incarceration itself, and strength through maintaining some control over aspects of their own lives (Johnson & Easterling, 2015). Deidentification is a form of avoidance and an adaptive strategy where adolescents distance themselves from and do not feel close to their incarcerated parent nor do they acknowledge any similarities between themselves and the incarcerated parent (Johnson &

Easterling, 2015). As noted by 14 year-old Selena, whose father has been incarcerated for multiple assaults since she was about seven years old, "I am nothing like him. He doesn't even know me or anything I'm interested in. He still thinks I'm this little girl. I don't care about him." The second strategy is desensitization to incarceration, which can be considered as a primary control strategy that takes the form of "normalizing or minimizing the situation" by not perceiving the incarceration as an issue or problem (Johnson & Easterling, 2015, p. 255). After being released and then re-incarcerated for another assault, Selena says about her father that "He can just stay there for all I care. It doesn't affect my life. I know lots of people whose dad is in jail. It's no big deal." The third strategy employed by adolescents is finding strength by maintaining some control over aspects of their own lives, also considered a type of control strategy (Johnson & Easterling, 2015). When 15 year-old Jerome's father was incarcerated for the third time for drug-related charges, Jerome became very focused on getting good grades in school. He notes, "I do NOT want to be like him. I can be different from him. I can do something with myself." In this way Jerome exerted some control over at least one aspect of his life. A secondary control category identified of finding strength and maintaining control involves "controlling the parental relationship" with the incarcerated parent (Johnson & Easterling, 2015). Both Selena and Jerome decided not to visit their fathers in prison and that they would figure out the relationship upon their release. This gave both adolescents the opportunity to define their contact and connection to their fathers, gaining a sense of empowerment over an otherwise disempowering situation. Typically control strategies are associated with better outcomes for adolescents as compared to disengagement or avoidance strategies (Compas, Connor-Smith, Saltzman, Thomsen, & Wadsworth, 2001; Johnson & Easterling, 2015).

RELOCATION

In recent years, relocation has become a more frequent occurrence in the lives of adolescents than in previous years. This may be due to parental employment issues for increased opportunity or a transfer, financial issues, or home and job loss due to natural disasters such as floods, hurricanes, tornadoes, and wildfires. Although many adolescents adjust to relocation, there are certainly those who do not. Vulnerability to relocation in adolescence is related to their developmental task of identity formation. Peer relationships have an impact on and help shape identity formation, and relocation removes adolescents from those very peers. Being the new kid in a new high school in a new city or town and perhaps new state adds increased pressure to both fit in and stand out, a stress-inducing adolescent task. The loss, grief, and possible trauma responses caused by relocation can prove difficult, if not insurmountable, for an adolescent.

Relocation Due to Parental Employment
Beginning as early as the late 20th century, the United States began to see a much more migratory and transitory society, with families relocating to follow employment opportunities related to transfers, layoffs, and the shutting down or reorganization of employers. Both real and perceived opportunities may be afforded employees who move from one job location to another. Entire geographic areas of the United States have been impacted as large employers such as steel mills and automobile plants have closed their doors, thus creating a large group of employees in need of opportunity. Many families found it necessary to relocate geographically to follow job possibilities. One of the results of a migratory society is the decrease in multigenerational families living together or near one another. For many adolescents, their earlier years were peopled with extended family members, and a parent's search and securing employment elsewhere causes them to experience multiple losses due to relocation. They no longer have their grandparents to spend time with or aunts, uncles, and cousins to visit, particularly when they feel misunderstood by their parents. Adolescents lose a naturally built-in and needed buffer to the natural individuation separation process they are undergoing with respect to their parents.

Ideally relocation would coincide with the beginning of a new school year; however, this is not always a possibility for the family. To walk into a new school and the already formed friendship and peer groups during the school year is awkward, embarrassing, stressful, and brings unwanted attention to an adolescent. This may have an impact on school performance, the ability and desire to make new friends, and an adolescent's developing and wavering sense of self. Much of an adolescent's ability to adapt to a new school environment is dependent on the inner resources of each adolescent as well as his past successes in navigating his previous high school environment.

Relocation Due to Financial Issues
Some families may decide to relocate due to financial issues that can span from not having enough money to maintain the current living arrangement to having more money to upgrade their living situation. When

families experience financial problems and are unable to pay the rent or mortgage, it may lead to eviction or loss of the house. There are a few possible solutions. The family moves in with extended family members, or they move from a house to an apartment or from an apartment to a hotel. An adolescent may lose his own bedroom and now has to share with siblings or other relatives, inevitably losing his privacy at a time when it is extremely important to have his own space to retreat to. Accompanying this relocation is often a move to a different school. Even if the relocation is within the same city but a different neighborhood, the school or school district may differ dramatically. As mentioned previously, entering a different school system is very stressful for adolescents.

Some families have the experience of an improvement or positive increase in their financial situation. This is the time when many families consider moving into a bigger house and/or a better school system. This may entail the family moving from leasing an apartment to purchasing a house or moving from one house to a bigger house in a more prestigious neighborhood. Again, an adolescent is confronted with relocation to a different school and away from the familiar and known. Either of these relocations due to financial issues can present a very powerful non-death loss for adolescents as they leave their friends, peers, and neighborhood.

Relocation Due to Natural Disaster

Adolescents who relocate after a natural disaster to a different city or different state from the one in which they originally lived report more trauma symptoms and depression as compared to those adolescents who were able to return to their home town or state (Blaze & Shwalb, 2009; Hansel, Osofsky, Osofsky, & Friedrich, 2013). Disoriented grief, a type of grief reaction posited by Malone, Pomeroy, and Jones (2011), describes the layers of loss created by natural disasters, which may be a component of the loss, grief, and trauma responses evidenced by adolescents who relocate with their families due to a natural disaster. There can be both death and non-death losses associated with natural disasters. Floods, hurricanes, tornadoes, and wildfires, to name a few, can produce layer upon layer of loss. Adolescents lose their homes, their possessions, and their place in the world. Much of what was familiar and known to them is gone forever. The four domains of disoriented grief include displacement, destruction, distress, and death. Adolescents are displaced as they experience both symbolic and concrete losses such as loss of family, loss of friends, loss of pets, and loss of identity. Destruction refers to loss of the family home, loss of belongings, and the loss of one's neighborhood.

Distress describes the emotional reaction of adolescents as they face the aftermath of a disaster. And of course, death loss can come in many forms. "Survivors may experience distress at witnessing traumatic events during the disaster, loss of dignity or hope, concern over health and injuries, and loss of time" (Malone, Pomeroy, & Jones, 2011, p. 257). Natural disasters most often cause many deaths, and the level of destruction is unfathomable. As a disaster survivor, adolescents are faced with a myriad of emotions to include feeling both fortunate and guilty at being alive, as well as anger, confusion, sadness, and shock. The ensuing loss, grief, and trauma can be on a grand scale, causing a state of bereavement overload that can last a long time. This is coupled with the loss of the security of the family as the adults in an adolescent's life struggle with the many layers of loss.

FRIENDSHIP LOSS

The loss or dissolution of friendship is an area rife with angst and pain for many adolescents. The relational world of the adolescent and her connections to friends has an important impact on her development of a sense of self. An adolescent's relational world is dominated largely by the peer group (Noppe & Noppe, 2004). The major task of adolescence is identity formation, with themes of separation and connectedness having primacy, making the peer group and the development and maintenance of friendships crucial components of this work. With friends, they get to try out who they are and who they want to be. They explore self-expression through clothing, music, use of social media, and involvement in extracurricular activities. The process of developing a sense of self along with self-expression is very much determined by the impressions and reactions of friends.

Friendship in adolescence is extremely important; it contributes to shaping social, emotional, and cognitive development, and it plays a significant role in developing the ability to handle a variety of psychosocial tasks (Oltjenbruns, 1996). Adolescents perceive themselves as members of the peer culture and view their peers, popular culture, and themselves as the support system that offers feedback and definition. Additionally, friendships provide the opportunity for adolescents to absorb other's perceptions (Steese et al., 2006). They begin to see that their viewpoint is not the only one, that there are other perspectives. They begin to see shades of gray in what previously appeared to be a black and white world differentiated by good and bad, right and wrong, true or false. This newly developed skill in seeing another's perspective affords them the ability to separate out the behavior from the person. They begin to become less judgmental of others. Yet there is absorption with sameness and difference among peers. They want to belong but do not want to be viewed as just like everyone else, and they certainly dislike standing out as too different for fear of being seen as odd, weird, or crazy.

Developing and maintaining close friendship relationships is important to both adolescent boys and adolescent girls. This process begins during the tween years, approximately nine to twelve years of age, peaking during middle school as the emergence of groups and cliques heightens. Of course these groups and cliques can continue into and throughout high school; however, many adolescents prefer connection and intimacy with a few close friends. These friendship relationships are the ones that offer meaning and depth to adolescents. These are the friends to whom they can turn not just for fun and during the good times but more importantly when they are sad, angry, confused, or scared. The expectation is that these friends understand their thoughts and feelings on a deep level, and they can trust them with their secrets, hopes, and fears. Sharing secrets and being openly vulnerable with one another is imperative between close adolescent friends. It sets the stage for developing intimate and deeply meaningful relationships in adulthood.

Friendship loss can occur due to circumstances outside the control of an adolescent, which may include a friend moving away or transferring to a different school. Typically, however, friendship loss is due to the dissolution of the relationship. This may be due to adolescents growing apart from one another or beginning to navigate different social circles and belong to other groups. If friends become part of social circles that have too many layers between them, then the friendship is in jeopardy. When Anita and Malia entered high school, their friendship shifted. According to 15 year-old Anita, Malia "Always tried to be part of the popular girls' group in middle school." During that time Malia hung on the fringes of the popular girls' group, not always included in their activities. In high school Malia succeeded in becoming a member of the most popular girls' group. Anita was definitely not one of the popular girls. She became more focused on academics, and actually hovered outside most of the high school groupings, belonging to none in particular. Malia would only socialize with Anita outside of school, calling her when she had a problem with a friend or a boyfriend. Since Anita had very few friends, she tolerated Malia's coldness at school and allowed their secret friendship. Anita had to decide if this was the kind of friend she wanted. Ultimately, the friendship became strained and ended, which saddened Anita and left her feeling alone and isolated.

Unlike a romantic breakup, being "dumped" or betrayed by a friend does not garner the same support from other friends. This is especially true if adolescent girls, such as Anita, do not belong to a clique or friendship group to whom they can turn for understanding and sorting through the ensuing thoughts and feelings. Friendship loss can be a very isolating and misunderstood experience. Both adolescent girls and adolescent boys crave the closeness and intimacy that a rich friendship can offer. Adolescent boys have been socialized by Western culture to deny or hide their painful feelings regarding loss of a boy friend for fear that they will be perceived or judged as gay or involved in a "bromance" (Way, 2011). Robert, a 17 year-old football player, talks about his best friend James of the past three years. "We talked about everything. Girls, football, teachers, college. And then my mom got sick about a year ago. James was totally there for me. I could tell him anything. I was scared. I told him that. And then something, I don't know, changed. Some guys in the locker room called us fags, that we were like a couple of girls talking all the time." Robert continued to describe the dissolution of his friendship with James. It appears that James was impacted by the other adolescent boys' judgment of their friendship, and shut it down. Robert shrugs it off, and stoically remarks, "I guess it ran its course." This experience erodes an adolescent's ability to trust, to take emotional risks toward the intimacy of friendship.

An important psychosocial task in developing friendship in adolescence involves taking an emotional risk in allowing oneself to become vulnerable to rejection, judgment, and betrayal. Yet the rewards of friendship entail closeness, intimacy, and trust, components desired by both adolescent girls and adolescent boys. Reactions from both adults and peers to adolescent friendship loss can tend to disenfranchise and minimize adolescents' feelings, leaving them unwilling to become vulnerable again. Adolescents need caring others, both adults and peers, to understand that the end of a friendship can be a painful and devastating experience of loss, grief, and even trauma.

ROMANTIC BREAKUP

One of the most stressful life events for an adolescent is when a romantic relationship comes to an end. More than half of adolescents have been involved in a romantic relationship during their high school years (Larson & Sweeten, 2012). Given an adolescent's natural narcissism, their first experiences with passionate attraction for another, and their still developing interpersonal skills that go into navigating that relationship, a romantic breakup can be a devastating loss characterized by an intense grief. It can be viewed as a major life change for an adolescent. Adults typically disenfranchise or minimize this loss, telling adolescents they are too young for it to count as a serious relationship, this is only the beginning of their dating lives, they disliked the boy or girl, and that there are "plenty more fish in the sea." This disenfranchising sentiment tends to discount and underestimate the intensity of an adolescent's thoughts and emotions in response to romantic loss. "Grief is further minimized for adolescents since they are erroneously perceived as incapable of experiencing both attachment and loss as intense emotional experiences" (Kaczmarek & Backlund, 1991, p. 253). The adults in adolescents' lives often do not take their romantic relationships seriously, assuming it is just the beginning of these experiences. A romantic breakup may appear relatively minor to adults, yet an adolescent can perceive it as a catastrophic, traumatic, and life-altering event. Adolescents enjoy the affiliative functions of dating such as spending time together, enjoying one another's companionship, and experiencing intimacy, passionate love, and attraction with someone special (Ha, Overbeek, Lichtwarck-Aschoff, & Engels, 2013). Adolescent loss and grief reactions in response to losing these valued qualities with a significant person can have a profound effect. In a study assessing common stressful life events and difficulties in adolescents, breaking up with a boyfriend or girlfriend was identified as the second most worried about issue, outranked only by parental separation or divorce (Low, Dugas, O'Loughlin, Rodriquez, Contreras, Chaiton, & O'Loughlin, 2012). These relationships are very important aspects of adolescent life. It is no surprise, then, that romantic involvement among adolescents and breaking up is associated with depression, anxiety, and conduct disorders (Davila, 2008; Low et al., 2012; Monroe, Rohde, Seeley, & Lewinsohn, 1999; Natsuaki, Biehl, & Ge, 2009). These ensuing disorders and struggles have an impact on adolescents' academic performance, identity development, sense of self-worth, and their familial and peer relationships. Poor adjustment to stressful events and problematic relationships during adolescence may evolve into mental health issues as they enter adulthood (Low et al., 2012). If not taken seriously by the adults and caring others in their lives, adolescents who experience difficult romantic breakups can be deleteriously affected for a long time.

Tanisha, an 18 year-old senior graduating and with plans to join the Army talked about her boyfriend of three years and their recent breakup. "We've known each other for years and I really and truly thought we would be together forever. Folks do meet their true loves at 15. We could finish each other's sentences and knew what the other was feeling. I just don't understand how he could do this. Be with another girl!? We pledged our love to one another. We're both joining the Army, the same Army. We have the same group of friends. We have the same interests, the same plans. I don't know what I'm gonna do now." Tanisha went on to describe an inability to concentrate, feelings of deep sadness, anxiety, irritability, low self-esteem, and an uncertainty about her future.

Romantic breakups during adolescence are typically sudden and unexpected, with very little time for preparation and adjustment. There is the tendency for adolescents to view a romantic relationship as their one true love, with fantasies of an eternal future together. Given that adolescents spend the majority of their time in the school environment, what would normally be a private loss and grief event rapidly becomes public knowledge. This is especially true due to the frequency and immediacy of adolescent digital natives' use of technology to share and broadcast news throughout the day. In addition to the public knowledge of her grief, an adolescent may see couples everywhere she looks, and possibly her ex-partner showing interest in or being with another romantic partner. An adolescent going through a romantic breakup may experience peers judging or avoiding her due to their own discomfort with feelings of grief, and with the uncertainty and insecurity of their own romantic relationships. Without the knowledge about or previous experience with grief related to a romantic breakup, adolescents may not know how to support a peer, and may conform to other peers' expectations and reactions (Rowling, 2002). This can lead to feelings of loneliness, isolation, embarrassment, low self-worth, and, as previously noted, anxiety and depression. These characteristics "are the perfect recipe for intense grief" during adolescence (Martin, 2002, p. 239). Add to this experience anything else occurring in an adolescent's life that could cause a grief overload or a triggering of previous loss, and school performance and conduct may be impacted.

Of particular challenge is the romantic breakup of same-sex adolescent couples. Adolescents who come out as homosexual during high school already run the risk of ridicule, judgment, and estrangement from both peers and adults. Those same adolescents who exhibit the courage to become involved in a same-sex romantic relationship during high school encounter the double risk of all that an adolescent romantic breakup entails as well as the possibility of negative remarks afterward. As Brendon, age 17, describes after his one-year relationship with Mark ended, "My parents said maybe now I should be with girls." Not only was the breakup minimized but the very nature of the relationship was negated and disenfranchised. Gay and lesbian adolescents who experience a romantic breakup experience a sort of double jeopardy, putting them at risk for the same characteristics mentioned above as well as the possibility of intrusive and severe depression and anxiety symptoms.

Parental support during an adolescent's experience of a romantic breakup can deter and decrease the persistence of depressive symptoms. In a study examining the relationship among romantic stress, adolescent depressive symptoms, and parental support, results indicate that even though romantic stress is linked to depression in adolescence, parental support, particularly in the form of maternal support, acts as a buffer for both adolescent boys and adolescent girls (Anderson, Salk, & Hyde, 2015). Typically adolescents have not developed the coping skills and resources necessary to meet the challenges posed by romantic stress and romantic breakup. This underscores the need for parental involvement throughout adolescence and most importantly as they learn to navigate interpersonal relationships. This can be difficult when adolescents present a sense of bravado as a way to hide their painful thoughts and feelings related to a romantic breakup and attempt to manage this loss alone.

CHAPTER 4

The Death of Loved Ones and Others

This chapter covers the death of loved ones and others in an adolescent's life, to include parental death, the death of a grandparent, sibling, friend/peer/classmate, or pet. For this book's purposes, the term *parent* will be used here to include any legal guardian who is in a parental role. Adolescence is a period of time when the meaning of death is typically contemplated. Adolescents contemplate both their own death and the deaths of others in their lives. The impact of death on adolescents, and the ways in which adolescents react to death-related issues, are determined and characterized by adolescent development and its tasks (Balk, 2014). Table 4.1 lists many types of death losses that an adolescent might encounter throughout this period of life.

DEATH OF A PARENT

Parental death has an unsurprising, yet unique, impact on adolescents. The normative and major developmental task of adolescence is that of separation and individuation from parents. Adolescents still need their

Table 4.1 Death Loss During Adolescence

Death Loss
Death of parent
Death of grandparent
Death of sibling
Death of other family member
Death of a friend or peer
Death of a teacher, coach, school personnel
Death of a pet
Death of a famous person

parents during this process as a safe haven to return to for a secure sense of anchoring and grounding. An adolescent's experience of a parent's death creates a complete, final, and irreversible separation, which may often be unanticipated and sudden (Hooyman & Kramer, 2006). It disturbs perceptions of and their still developing skills in interpersonal relationships, which may result in increased isolation and decreased support at a time when relationships with peers, parents, and teachers are critical to adjustment, well-being, and identity development. In a study aimed at comparing the adjustment of adolescents who experienced the death of a parent with those who experienced parental divorce, in addition to comparison with a control group, results indicate that both types of loss impair the intrapersonal adjustment of adolescents (Servaty & Hayslip, 2001). This refers to the ways in which adolescents develop a sense of self or identity, about who they are and who they are becoming. This study explored adjustment difficulties as measured on the Hopkins Symptom Checklist, which includes subscales of somatization or physical grief responses, obsessive-compulsive activity, interpersonal sensitivity, depression, and anxiety. In comparison to the control group and the parental divorce group, adolescents experience more adjustment difficulties following a parental death, and adolescent girls in particular score higher than adolescent boys on all subscales, but significantly on somatization subscales, indicating more bodily complaints or physical grief responses among girls (Servaty & Hayslip, 2001). Physical grief responses may include stomachaches, headaches, sleep disturbances, joint pain, and being ill more often. Additional results indicate feelings of inadequacy and inferiority; difficulties with social competence assessed as participation in activities, working, or getting along with others; as well as school functioning (Servaty & Hayslip, 2001).

In a yearlong study following 11 adolescents, aged 13 to 18, who experienced the death of a parent, Harris (1991) noted high levels of sleep disturbance, poor concentration, and deterioration of school performance. Some of these adolescents also struggled with depression, alcohol abuse, skipping school, delinquency, and school failure. In a similar study of the impact of parental death, Gray (1987) assessed grief in adolescents aged 12 to 19 and found a link between lower depression scores and high levels of informal social support, a good relationship with the surviving parent prior to death of the other parent, a balanced personality style, and the presence of religious beliefs.

Worden and Silverman (1996) conducted the Child Bereavement Study to investigate 70 children and adolescents over two years who experienced the death of a parent. At the two-year follow-up, the bereaved adolescents scored higher on levels of anxiety, depression, and social withdrawal as compared to the adolescent control group.

The death of a parent or guardian creates an indelible mark upon the developing adolescent, a sort of branding that carries into adulthood. The adolescent is forever changed, wondering if her deceased parent would like her and understand the young woman she is becoming. Jennie was 13 when her mother died of lung cancer. She is now 16 and states, "I look around and I see all these other girls with their moms and I just want to be one of them. I know I have my dad and my brothers and sisters, but I just keep wondering what it would be like to have her here all the time. I wonder if I would argue with her and get mad at her. I wonder if she would like me now."

Themes that emerged from research on adolescents' response to impending parental death include a sense of isolation, the difficulty of living with uncertainty, the need for support rather than protection from the difficulties that lie ahead, support within the school, the preference for information and involvement as opposed to delay and deception, truth as an essential desire, and talking about dying as a risk of foretelling its occurrence (Chowns, 2014). A research study that looked at final conversations between adolescents and dying loved ones identified three themes of advice that include the importance of confirming and maintaining the relationship with the dying, staying positive about and present with the experience, and the benefits of using one's support system (Keeley & Generous, 2014). Additionally, communication and conversation between an adolescent and her dying parent is important. The time before her parent's death allows for specific communication themes to emerge that may include messages about love, messages about their relationship and the adolescents' developing identity, and messages related to both religious and spiritual beliefs (Keeley & Generous, 2014).

Adolescents often feel a sense of isolation as they go through the impending death of a parent. They are set apart from their peers. As discussed in chapter two, adolescents often do not want to be marked as different from their peers and friendship group. However, the experience of living with a terminally ill parent does just that. Adolescents with siblings often do not share information or knowledge with one another

(Chowns, 2014); this is dependent on differing age ranges as well as family roles. Parentified adolescents are those who are either assigned a more parental role by the other adults in their life, or they take on this over-functioning role as a way of coping. Juanita, age 16, is the oldest of four children. She helps her mother with her younger siblings, often doing the majority of the work, while her father is dying of liver cancer. "I tell the little ones that it's gonna be okay, that we're gonna be okay. They have me, you know?" Adolescents who are only children may feel even more isolated, having no one in the family with whom to share the loss. Additionally, an adolescent without siblings may also experience his still living but grieving parent as not very present or attentive to him, which adds to his loss. Adolescents experience a great amount of stress and helplessness living with the uncertainty of their parent's anticipated or impending death. They worry about what life without that parent will be like, who they will become without that parent, and do not really know what to do or how to act in the present. As 15 year-old Michael states while witnessing and awaiting his mother's death due to breast cancer, "I've never done this before. I'm not even sure what I'm supposed to do except be with her and wait. Should I go to the football games?" This questioning of what should be a normal adolescent life may alter his perspective about life, his involvement in activities both in and out-side of school, as well as his connection to others.

Although some adolescents can appear more mature and adult-like, they still need support from family and friends, both in the home and out-side of the home. Support can be useful coming from teachers, coaches, and counselors. Support can look different given the needs of each indi-vidual adolescent.

Chowns (2014) found that some adolescents discussed the need to be given space by teachers, that they at times needed a bit of alone time or quiet time at the end of a class, or some time with peers and friends. Many adolescents express the need for support from the school in the form of teachers understanding when homework is turned in late if at all, and that the work may not be up to par. Loss and grief have an impact on an adolescent's ability to concentrate both in the classroom and at home when attempting homework. Adolescents want the school community to understand and care about them as they face the difficulty of their parent dying.

Reactions from friends can be either helpful or hurtful. After 15 year-old Jenna's father died in a car accident due to drinking and driving, friends made remarks about him causing it. "These girls, they said he had it coming to him, that what did he expect? That was really harsh." Mark, who turned 16 the day after his mother died, stated, "A friend said I know how you feel. But how can he know? He thinks that 'cause his parents got divorced he knows how this feels. It doesn't even compare."

Another theme that emerged from Chowns' (2014) research is that adolescents want to be involved and prefer information about their parent's prognosis. They want accurate information and to be informed early in the process. They do not want delayed information or misinformation, but desire truthfulness above all else. However, adolescents may also express concern that talking about a parent's impending death is a way of foretelling its occurrence or "making it happen" (Chowns, 2014, p. 29).

DEATH OF A GRANDPARENT

A grandparent's death is often the first familial experience that an adolescent has with the concept of dying, death, funerals, and, depending on the circumstances, with an anticipated or a sudden death. Approximately 90% of adolescents in high school, particularly those in the 11th and 12th grades, experience the death of a grandparent (Oltjenbruns, 1996). The death of a grandparent occurs within the normal course of life, or the typical cycle of life where elders die before younger people. However, the death of a grandparent tends to increase death anxiety in adolescents. Ideas and thoughts related to death become prevalent in the mind of an adolescent following the death of a grandparent. This may be the first time that an adolescent actually entertains the idea of his own death. He may also begin to think about the very real chance of his outliving his own parents. Adolescents may grieve intensely depending on the closeness of family ties to their grandparent (Ens & Bond, 2007). Additionally, the relationship between a grandparent and an adolescent may be a significant and important aspect of both their lives. These two generations may share similar interests and insights, with the grandparent perhaps offering a safe and secure emotional space, which may differ from that of the adolescent's relationship with his parents. Given the newly emerging developmental issues of adolescence regarding individuation and separation from parents, an adolescent may find comfort and ease in connection with a grandparent. Some adolescents have a deeply bonded relationship with a grandparent. Hence, the death of this grandparent and the change in the bond can have a powerful impact on an adolescent, creating a deep sense of loss and grief. This can also be true for adolescents who live in multigenerational house-holds, where a grandparent's death creates an absence in the immediate household. The adolescent may have relied on the grandparent for advice and guidance, and possibly as a buffer between the adolescent and his parents.

The death of a grandparent also gives an adolescent insight into his own parents' grieving styles and ways of reacting to the death of one of their parents. He may watch closely to learn about both cultural and gender-specific ways of grieving. He may take his cues from his parents regarding how to act, how to feel, and how to show or not show his grief. Additionally, the death of a grandparent may have an impact on his grieving parents' ability and capacity to support him through this loss, since they may be consumed by their own grief. It is often a time for families to grieve together as a unit, which can offer an adolescent support from extended family members. This is especially helpful as his parents grieve their loss.

DEATH OF A SIBLING

Regardless of closeness or tension, siblings offer lifelong companionship and rivalry unmatched by any other relationship. Brothers and sisters may disagree, argue, and have differing perspectives when it comes to family events and memories, or they may be bonded in their similar perspectives and experiences, sharing life events in ways that other relationships cannot match. Whatever their relationship, there is a historical connection between siblings that does not compare to that of friends, partners, or spouses. To lose a sibling to death during adolescence, a time of change that already has an impact on the sibling relationship, causes an adolescent to feel numerous emotions. This can complicate a period of time when adolescents experience emotional growing pains as their range of feeling and tolerating emotions expands. The death of a sibling causes an array of feelings such as confusion, shock, guilt (to include survivor guilt), fear, anger, and loneliness, with depression and anxiety being described as the most predominant emotional reactions (Balk, 2009). Often family, friends, and the community focus on the parent who is grieving the loss of a child rather than on a surviving sibling, who becomes a forgotten mourner. The focus is on the parental grief, which is given more com-passion than the pain experienced by a surviving sibling. The impact of sibling death during adolescence tends to be underestimated. An adolescent may have lost a sibling who was both a best friend and confidant, leaving him feeling alone and abandoned. Close friends cannot take the place of a sibling, nor can cousins or other family members. For some adolescents, striving to differentiate from a sibling, to define an identity different and apart from their sibling, may have been of paramount importance. Losing this sibling can complicate the crucial adolescent task of identity formation (Hooyman & Kramer, 2006). Additionally, going through adolescence and into young adulthood means that the surviving adolescent will travel that developmental journey alone without his sibling to whom he may have turned for advice, or with whom he shared his thoughts, fears, excitement, trepidation, and hopes and plans for the future. Now he faces an uncertain future without his sibling.

A secondary or additional loss for an adolescent whose sibling has died is if exhausted and emotionally depleted parents are not available, attentive, or responsive to his needs. This can add to his experience of loneliness and abandonment, not knowing to whom he can turn for emotional support and assistance in making sense of a senseless loss. This is especially poignant if it was an unexpected and sudden sibling death. His parents are also experiencing many of the same emotions, such as shock, guilt, anger, and an unfathomable sadness. If an adolescent's sibling had been struggling with an illness, then his parents were busy and absorbed with caring for his sibling and trying to balance a household. Abandonment and loneliness is a common feeling experienced by adolescents with a dying sibling.

An adolescent often hides or camouflages his feelings in response to concerns about his parents' well-being after the death of a sibling, as a way of rescuing the family from continued emotional chaos and devastation (Balk, 2014). He may avoid any discussion or conversation with parents about his sibling's death in order to diminish their worries and sadness, and put up a seemingly strong front. Other adolescents may become emotional caretakers of their bereaved parents, taking on far more responsibilities than typical for an adolescent. As 16 year-old Josh states about his 13 year-old sister's death by suicide, "I just had to be strong for my mom. She was so torn up, a mess. I couldn't just fall apart. I had to be there for her." This may replace his involvement in other adolescent-related activities both in school and outside of school. He may shun other relationships as he exerts energy and spends time as his parent's emotional caretaker. This can have an impact on his future relationships with others if his role of emotional caretaker solidifies as part of his identity.

There has been much discussion and speculation in the literature about the impact of a sibling's death by suicide on adolescents. Many parents are concerned about surviving siblings, fearful that they too will make a suicide attempt. It is not typically the suicide itself that leads to issues or problems for the adolescent but family functioning prior to and after the sibling's death (Cerel & Aldrich, 2011). This relates to the emotional availability and responsiveness of parents to the surviving adolescent. Many factors or mediators contribute to the well-being of an adolescent whose sibling died by suicide. These include interpersonal skills, the existence and use of a support system, intrapersonal strengths, coping techniques, and the adolescent's overall functioning prior to his sibling's death. The loss, grief, and trauma responses associated with a sibling's death by suicide may include feeling stigmatized, judged, a sense of embarrassment, shame, guilt, rejection, and a profound isolation, as well as lowered academic performance. "These characteristics reflect a combination of an intense grief response overlaid with a trauma response" (Jordan & McIntosh, 2011, p. 229). Sibling death by suicide is certainly a traumatic event in the lives of both the family and the adolescent.

Regardless of the cause of a sibling's death, family functioning both prior to and after an adolescent's sibling's death is the most important mediator or factor influencing adolescent adjustment and well-being. This is most characterized by the degree of family coherency. Greater family coherency involves close attachment between the adolescent and family members, as evidenced by the adolescent's frequency of communication and ability to discuss important issues with family members. Adolescents living in these family environments tend to adapt to their loss and grief over time with a subsiding of distress. They tend to have people with whom they can talk about their thoughts, feelings, and behavior in response to the death of a sibling. Those with less family coherency experience more emotional distance and either rarely or never discuss important issues and feelings related to the sibling's death and its impact on the surviving adolescent. The emotional reaction most predominantly felt by these adolescents is confusion (Balk, 2014). They typically guess or make presumptions about appropriate grief reactions, and they do not know what to do with the accompanying thoughts and feelings.

Above all, positive and consistent parenting is crucial for adolescents who have experienced the death of a sibling. Parents can model ways of maintaining continuing bonds by keeping linking objects, such as keeping photographs in the house or having photos on their cell phones and pictures in their wallet. Keeping objects that were important to that child as reminders is important. Parents can support adolescents by including them in deciding what objects to keep and how to display or maintain them. Parents can support and normalize the maintenance of continuing bonds by sharing with their adolescent about internal conversations they have with the deceased sibling (Balk, 2009). This sharing is especially beneficial since adolescents often worry that they are abnormal or crazy for having these same internal conversations.

DEATH OF A PET

Many adolescents have had the pleasure of sharing the household with a pet, some since childhood. The length of time a pet has been in the life of an adolescent and the degree of human-pet connection between an adolescent and her pet are factors that have an impact on her when her pet dies. Pets are often perceived as members of the family and offer the opportunity for mutual affection, a sense of intimacy, and, certainly as anyone who has had the joy of a pet in their lives knows, the experience of unconditional love. "For many adolescents, pets serve as silent counselors, best friends, and even surrogate siblings" (Brown, Richards, & Wilson, 1996, p. 505). An adolescent can have a day at school full of disappointments and social awkwardness, and arrive home to find her dog excited to see her. The bond between an adolescent and a pet can be strong and deep. Given this, and that there is a connection between attachment and grief (Bowlby, 1980), the grief that ensues after the death of a pet can be a devastating, even traumatic, experience for an adolescent. This death loss must be treated as seriously as any family member's death, because the grief is real and can be very powerful. For some adolescents, this is their first real experience with the death of a loved one. Pets, just like people, can die suddenly and unexpectedly or endure a long illness. Adolescents need the emotional space to work through the grief process just as they do when a person dies (Meyers, 2002).

Continuing bonds is a concept that relates to coping with the loss, grief, and trauma associated with the death loss of loved ones, to include both people and pets. Although there is a permanent physical separation, adolescents can feel emotionally connected to their deceased pet. In a study to evaluate the degree of connection between people and their deceased pet, continuing bonds expressions were described in the form of recalling fond memories and thoughts of their pet, holding onto or using belongings specific to their pet in order to maintain a sense of closeness, reminiscing with others about their pet, learning lessons from or being positively influenced by their pet, having thoughts of being reunited with their pet, having dreams about their pet, and sensing the presence and continued connection with their pet (Carmack & Packman, 2011).

A few weeks after his dog was run over by a car and died, 13 year-old Tom notes, "Sometimes I feel him at my feet when I'm at my computer doing homework. It's like he's there. I can even smell him and hear him licking. I really miss him. I even reached down to pet him one time." Normalizing the feelings and behaviors as continuing bonds can be beneficial to adolescents who may believe they are abnormal, crazy, or just plain strange.

DEATH OF A FRIEND OR PEER

Friends and peers play a central role in how adolescents deal with various psychosocial tasks, and the death of a peer may delay successful completion of those tasks (Oltjenbruns, 1996). Adolescents receive feedback from friends and peers about their thoughts, feelings, and behavior. They learn from one another how to dress, how to act with one another, when and how to date, what music to listen to, what movies to watch, which books are interesting, and more importantly, gain some perspective on how they are perceived by others. They need friends and peers with whom they can try out who they are and who they are becoming. The death of a friend or peer can upset or complicate, but most certainly have an impact on, identity formation, which may already be unstable (O'Brien et al., 1991).

Adolescents have not developed the social or emotional maturity to fully incorporate and process bereavement into a coherent worldview (Rowling, 2002). Although some adolescents have endured multiple grief, loss, and trauma experiences, and some may even present as mature beyond their years, they are still developmentally and emotionally adolescents. The sudden or violent death of a peer and the ensuing impact of loss, grief, and trauma have too often become part of an adolescent's life in the 21st century. Estimates of adolescents who report past-year death of a friend range upward from 20% (Rheingold et al., 2004), with earlier studies showing that 40% of adolescents experienced the death of a close friend (Ewalt & Perkins, 1979) and that 87% of adolescents experienced the death of a peer (Schachter, 1991). The majority of adolescent loss and grief studies focus on adolescent responses to the death of a parent (Servaty & Hayslip, 2001; Tyson-Rawson, 1996) or adolescent sibling bereavement (Balk, 1983, Bearman & Moody, 2004; Hogan & DeSantis, 1996). Few studies look at the impact of the death of a friend (Chapman, 2003: Noppe & Noppe, 2008; Oltjenbruns, 1996; Rheingold et al., 2004; Sklar & Hartley, 1990; Webb, 2002), and even fewer on the impact that peer death has on adolescents (Dyregrov, Gjestad, Wikander, & Vigerust, 1999; Melhem, Day, Shear, Day, Reynolds, & Brent, 2004; O'Brien et al., 1991; Ringler & Hayden, 2000).

There are more similarities than differences between adolescent loss, grief, and trauma experiences following the death of a family member and the death of a friend (Lurie, 1993). These findings suggest that loss, grief, and trauma reactions in response to the death loss of a close friend are similar to those of the death loss of a family member. Therefore, much of the documented loss, grief, and trauma reactions among adolescents in response to the death of a parent or sibling can be utilized in examining the loss, grief, and trauma reactions to the death of a peer. These reactions may include physical, social, emotional, and cognitive responses to loss, grief, and trauma. The death of a friend or peer during adolescence is perceived by developmental theorists and researchers as a potentially devastating and life-changing event that can create additional stress for an adolescent who has yet to resolve issues related to his or her identity (Balk, 1996; Rosen, 1991). In a study of 53 adolescents who experienced the death of a friend or peer, most reported feeling a range of emotional responses such as sadness, disbelief, surprise, shock, anger, and confusion as well as numbness, fear, and guilt (Schachter, 1991). McNeil, Silliman, and Swihart (1991) studied the reactions of 94 high school students 18 months after the death of a popular classmate to determine patterns of immediate grief and coping responses. This exploratory study found that adolescents tend to hide or camouflage their feelings from adults and from one another. These feelings include ongoing anger, distress, and confusion regarding the peer's death. It is difficult to determine what adolescents need from the adults in their lives when loss, grief, and trauma reactions are hidden or camouflaged.

A study investigating the impact of loss, trauma exposure, and mental health on adolescents found that the death of a friend was related to depression, posttraumatic stress disorder, and substance abuse/dependence (Rheingold et al., 2004). The past-year death of a friend also predicts past-year substance abuse/dependence. Oltjenbruns (1996) notes that grief following the death of a friend or peer can be viewed as disenfranchised and often includes a great sense of guilt. The loss, grief, and trauma reactions of adolescents may be complicated and significantly impacted by the fact that most peer deaths are sudden and viewed as preventable. These deaths are typically caused by accidents, homicides, or suicides (Barrett, 1996). Loss, grief, and trauma reactions can affect relationships with other friends, leading to enhanced feelings of estrangement, isolation, and a prolonged grief.

Adolescents tend to seek out one another when they have experienced the death of a friend or peer and may feel most comfortable talking with other adolescents who had been close to the deceased. Yet simultaneously, they can feel different from and misunderstood by their peers (Ringler & Hayden, 2000). These feelings are reinforced if peers are judgmental and insensitive to the adolescent's loss, grief, and trauma responses. Adolescents may feel discomfort talking with parents about feelings, often disappointed in their parents' reactions (O'Brien et al., 1991; Servaty-Seib, 2009). Many adolescents expect more support from parents than they actually receive. Parents are unsure how to react to their adolescent, especially if the deceased peer was not a best friend. Again, when adolescents hide or camouflage their loss, grief, and trauma responses, it is difficult for their parents to provide the needed support. The disenfranchised nature of adolescent grief is a phenomenon "that is shaped fundamentally by grieving rules of parents, other adults, and peers, all of whom create the grieving norms of an adolescent's world" (Rowling, 2002, p. 276). Many adolescents guess at what the grieving norms are and watch to see what they should be doing, how they should be feeling and behaving, and whether or not to even cry. Adolescents are often perceived as resilient and not seriously affected by the loss (Ringler & Hayden, 2000). Adults may not recognize the severity of this loss to an adolescent. The adolescent's perception of lack of parental support makes it difficult to find people they can trust and with whom to talk about the death of their friend or peer.

Adolescents live intensely in the present, and the experience of the death of a friend or peer causes them to unexpectedly look into the future at the possibility of their own death (Kandt, 1994). This is an unfamiliar concept, since most adolescents do not have as many experiences with death and loss as do adults. An adolescent's sense of safety and security about the world and ongoing relationships may be skewed as a result of the death of a friend or peer (Saltzman et al., 2002). They may begin to perceive the world as an unsafe place, and that building friendships and peer relationships is a precarious endeavor that could end in devastating loss. This is especially true given that the majority of adolescent deaths are sudden, providing no time for preparation for this loss.

Death of a Friend or Peer by Suicide

Suicide is the second leading cause of death, at 17.1%, of all deaths among adolescents in the United States (Centers for Disease Control and Prevention, 2013). The main methods used are with firearms (45.3%), by suffocation (37.7%), poisoning (8.6%), and intentional falling (3%). Bearman and Moody (2004) investigated the relationship between friendships and suicidality among male and female adolescents by analyzing the friendship data on over 13,000 adolescents from the National Longitudinal Survey of Adolescent Health. This data set includes adolescents from private, religious, and public high schools located in urban, suburban, and rural areas. Their results found that having a friend who committed suicide tended to increase suicidal ideation among both males and females, but socially isolated adolescent girls, as well as girls who were not part of social networks, had significantly increased suicidal thoughts. They suggest that the most effective intervention for girls is to transform the structure of their friendships by increasing involvement in extracurricular activities and joining clubs, thus decreasing their loneliness and isolation (Bearman & Moody, 2004).

In a longitudinal study that included 146 friends and acquaintances of 26 suicide victims, interviews at 6, 12 to 18, and 36 months after the peer's suicide yielded results that adolescents experience symptoms of traumatic grief reactions that follow a discernable path (Melhem et al., 2004). Traumatic grief, a syndrome distinct from depression and anxiety, is exhibited by symptoms that include poor physical health, crying, numbness, preoccupation with the deceased peer, sadness, yearning and searching for the deceased peer, and suicidal ideation. The researchers found the likelihood of developing traumatic grief was independent of depression. This study recommends clinicians and other caring adults to be alert to the occurrence of traumatic grief reactions among adolescents and the need to address them in treatment approaches.

The death of a peer due to suicide may cause grief reactions that differ from loss due to other causes of death. Adolescents, as well as adults, often attempt an emotional autopsy, trying to figure out what caused their peer to die by suicide. Rumors run rampant throughout a high school or community as adolescents rapidly connect with one another about their speculations. For adolescents struggling with depression, anxiety, substance use and abuse, and problems that seem to have no solution, a peer's death by suicide may cause them to contemplate their own intentional death. In a therapy setting, when asked about this, these adolescents will admit to suicidal ideation as well as the possibility of having made an unsuccessful attempt that no one knows about. It is important to provide and make available ongoing support to adolescents in schools and communities that experience the death of an adolescent due to suicide.

DEATH IN THE SCHOOL

Typically deaths that affect the school community are unexpected and unanticipated. There are profound effects on adolescent survivors of school community deaths that result from diseases and accidents or intentionally inflicted death due to homicide, suicide, or interpersonal violence (Hill & Foster, 1996). These types of deaths may include the sudden death of a peer or teacher due to an accident, homicide, or suicide or an anticipated death of a peer or teacher due to illness and disease. These death occurrences also include the unfortunate but real occurrence of violence within the school community such as stabbings and mass shootings that result in deaths. The school community offers an ideal environment in which to acknowledge the loss, grief, and trauma experiences of adolescents and to support them both individually and in groups. Schools can also develop, maintain, and manage plans for confronting critical loss, grief, and trauma situations (Rowling, 2002). School-based programs or postventions may be the response utilized to ease student reactions to the traumatic death of a classmate or teacher. There is a preponderance of literature that describes the theoretical basis, design, objectives, and format for implementing postvention groups (Catone & Schatz, 1991; Hill & Foster, 1996; Komar, 1994; Rickgarn, 1987; Rickgarn, 1996; Stevenson, 2002). There are also numerous postvention programs that all aim for a similar outcome to "minimize negative effects and build on the growth-enhancing potential available in all crises" (Hill & Foster, 1996, p. 258). Most postvention programs focus on reducing adolescent posttraumatic symptoms and increasing resilience-supporting factors, but with diverse approaches. Hill and Foster (1996) propose a postvention framework that all schools follow in developing a plan, to include:

- Designate a leader who will notify the postvention team members of the crisis
- Quickly manage dissemination of public information, that is, notify the media
- Postvention team meets immediately and includes custodial family members in the planning
- Notify teachers and other school personnel about crisis and the ensuing plan

- Inform the students using a preplanned process of small groups, not a large assembly
- Immediately provide small group and individual counseling
- Provide supportive consultation to parents and families
- Provide supportive consultation for the support staff
- Assess and make necessary and immediate referrals for adolescents identified as at-risk
- Provide adequate and careful follow-up, which may include ongoing small group and individual counseling

This framework can apply to all school settings, with variations dependent on each community's resources. However, it is imperative and forward thinking to have a detailed plan in place and ready to be implemented in response to any school community crisis.

CHAPTER 5

Gender Differences

There are differences in the characteristics of adolescent girl relationships and the characteristics of adolescent boy relationships. There are distinct differences in the ways in which they experience, communicate, and process the development and maintenance of connection with others. These differences can be attributed to the ways in which adolescent girls and adolescent boys inherently manage or cope with the distress associated with loss, grief, and trauma based on gender role socialization. The feelings may be similar yet the ways in which each gender expresses them can vary.

Much of the gender differences in grieving patterns can be attributed to social norms that tend to view gender in set binary roles of male and female. These roles are often fostered by familial and cultural values and patterns and are learned early in life. However, these differences beg the question regarding the role society, culture, and families play in shaping gender-specific grief reactions. "Gender role socialization becomes a major influence in, among other aspects, the expressions of grief and adaptation to loss" (Doka & Martin, 2010, pp. 125–126). Gendered grieving patterns in adolescence may be based on adolescent girls' and adolescent boys' relationship characteristics and the ways in which they develop and maintain their connections with close friends and peer groups.

ADOLESCENT GIRL RELATIONSHIPS

Adolescent girls relate to their friends and develop relationships in ways that differ from those developed by adolescent boys. They adopt connection-oriented goals, are empathetic, and tend toward interpersonal concerns. Many adolescent girls describe having one or two best friends, close friends, and acquaintances (O'Brien et al., 1991). As girls transition from middle school to high school, they often move into larger schools with greater potential for meeting like-minded friends, as well as the very real possibility of becoming lost and invisible in a more crowded environment. Those adolescent girls who maximize their potential for friendship during high school thrive on developing authentic connection to others, and they are apt to internalize rich emotional relationships with friends (Jordan, 2003). Many adolescent girls become emotionally involved in the lives of a wide range of people or social networks, and these connections with others are a central organizing feature in their psychological makeup (Brown & Gilligan, 1992). Their sense of self is developed primarily through their relationships with others. Adolescent girls tend to be emotionally expressive and highly empathetic and gravitate toward seeking out support from friends and peers. By seeking support, especially when loss, grief, and trauma experiences occur in their lives, adolescent girls increase the likelihood of receiving reassurance that problems are solvable and that they will not be overwhelmed by these problems. This support decreases the negative aspects of loss, grief, and trauma that can plague adolescent girls, such as excessive worrying, sadness, anxiety, and depression. The friendships that girls develop in adolescence offer a sense of closeness, affection and caring, trust, loyalty, a sense of security, an acceptance about who they are, validation and normalization of thoughts and feelings, an enhancement of their worth, and nurturance. These characteristics of adolescent girls' friendships may act as a buffer from the distress and negative thoughts and feelings associated with loss, grief, and trauma experiences.

However, there is a cost. Adolescent girls' heightened ability for empathy exposes them to evaluation from their peers, worry about that same perceived or real evaluation, feelings of hopelessness and shame when negatively judged, peer stress, and a tendency to ruminate about or overthink their problems, which can lead to anxiety and depression (Rose & Rudolph, 2006). Greater concerns about being evaluated and approved by others can contribute to emotional problems, such as anxiety and depression. Adolescent girls tend to worry about the status of their relationships and can experience jealousy with friendships. Distress over abandonment and friendship breakup, and over friends' relationships with others, real or perceived, tends to add to internalizing symptoms such as lowered self-worth and anxiety. With higher levels of empathy, adolescent girls have a greater tendency to experience stress and distress within the context of dyadic friendships and to vicariously experience the distress and problems of others who are members of their social network. Adolescent girls tend to perceive interpersonal stress in general and relational or social victimization in particular as more stressful or hurtful as compared to boys. "Girls' greater exposure to a wider variety of personal and vicarious stressful peer events and circumstances may contribute to their heightened vulnerability to emotional difficulties" (Rose & Rudolph, 2006, p. 120). This becomes more pronounced in adolescence, and it may contribute to what many perceive and label as "girl drama."

ADOLESCENT BOY RELATIONSHIPS

Adolescent boys tend to interact in groups of peers and are characterized by an activity-focused style. Yet they also develop deep close male friendships based on trust and loyalty, which challenges the touted gender stereotype of invulnerability. Friendships among adolescent boys play a critical role in their ability to develop and sustain healthy and intimate relationships both in adolescence and into adulthood. Without these close and deep friendships, adolescent boys may feel alienated and lonely, and appear shut down emotionally and inexpressive. If they have no outlet for expressing emotions such as disappointment or hurt feelings related to loss, grief, and trauma except through socially sanctioned action-oriented activities such as sports and other physical endeavors, then these powerful feelings may develop into anger and aggression. Yet the cost for outwardly promoting close male friendships is to be perceived, judged, and labeled as "girlish or gay" (Oransky & Maracek, 2009). This perception among adolescent boys becomes more pronounced and prevalent as boys move from early to late adolescence.

Adolescent boys in peer groups may foster more self-promoting behavior that serves to elevate their status in the dominance hierarchy (Way, 2011). It is not uncommon to see adolescent boys in groups using humor as a coping skill, and making light of stressful situations. The ability to make light of problems may buffer some adolescent boys from dwelling on and worrying about problems, which may protect them from the emotional distress associated with loss, grief, and trauma, particularly anxiety and depression.

Adolescent boys have the capacity for friendship connection that is based on mutual trust, a sense of safety, and the ability to talk deeply. They can be "acutely attuned to the emotional nuances in their friendships" and tend to value intimacy (Way, 2011, p. 92). Adolescent boys want to be known and understood in their friendships, and to be accepted for who they are. It is also important for them to develop connection with other adolescent boys they can depend on for support, sharing feelings, and talking about problems. Their trusted friendships often develop alongside their involvement in mutual interests such as participating in and watching sports; listening to and playing music; talking about and playing video games, particularly interactive multiplayer games; and academic-related endeavors such as being on the debate team and belonging to various clubs. This mutuality increases their likelihood of discovering other adolescent boys of like mind with whom they can develop the trust imperative for having intimate conversations and sharing "deep secrets" (Way, 2011).

DIFFERENT WAYS OF GRIEVING

Based on socially prescribed and stereotypic perceptions of gender differences in friendships, it is no surprise that there are differences in how females and males are expected to grieve. The expected loss, grief, and trauma reaction of females in Western society is to readily express their feelings, whereas males are expected to put on an emotionally stoic face. When adolescents do not behave in gender expected ways of grieving, they are often negatively judged by other adolescents and adults. When 15 year-old Benita wanted to join a loss and grief group for adolescent girls at her school, the girls who knew her did not want her to participate. "She cannot be part of our group. She just doesn't feel the right way. She doesn't cry. She's not sad. She doesn't care!" She was rejected and judged due to her perceived inability to grieve, based on her not readily expressing her emotions as prescribed by the accepted and stereotypic female norms.

The impact of loss, grief, and trauma on adolescents involves a number of physical, social, emotional, and cognitive grief and trauma responses (Balk, 2008; O'Brien et al., 1991). However, these responses in adolescent girls tend to differ from those experienced, or at least expressed, by adolescent boys (Chapman, 2003; Fleming & Balmer, 1996; Malone, 2012). Adolescent girls are more likely than adolescent boys to experience a prolonged and intense loss, grief, and trauma reaction, and to score higher on measures of the previously mentioned negative outcomes in response to loss, grief, and trauma (Malone, 2012; Servaty & Hayslip, 2001). This may be attributed to the fact that adolescence is an extremely vulnerable time period in a female's life due to the intense physical, emotional, cognitive, and relational changes that take place during puberty as she transitions from childhood to adulthood (Kling, Hyde, Showers, & Buswell, 1999; Noppe & Noppe, 2004; Ringler & Hayden, 2000). Additionally, adolescent girls are very attentive to and expressive regarding their emotions, as well as to the reactions and feelings of those around them. They tend to more passively and repetitively focus on distress, and use emotions to cope, which creates a very stressful reaction to loss, grief, and trauma. As compared to adolescent boys, adolescent girls express the need for more time to overcome the death of a classmate and that the deceased peer means more to them (Dyregrov et al., 1999). Bearman and Moody (2004) found that socially isolated girls have substantially increased suicidal ideation following the suicide of a peer. Additionally, the degree of bonding with a pet tends to be greater for girls than boys, as is the intensity of their grief responses to the death of a pet (Brown et al., 1996).

A study based on a nationally representative sample of 4,023 adolescents indicated that girls (23%) are more likely than boys (19%) to experience the death of a friend or peer within a one-year time frame (Rheingold et al., 2004). This speaks to the larger social networks that adolescent girls tend to construct around themselves. In comparison to a control group and a parental divorce group, adolescents in general experience more adjustment difficulties following a parental death, and adolescent girls in particular score higher than adolescent boys on all subscales, but significantly on somatization subscales, indicating more bodily complaints or physical grief responses among girls (Servaty & Hayslip, 2001). The results of a study involving adolescent girls who experienced the death of a peer indicate that physical grief responses take longer to resolve or lessen than social, emotional, or cognitive grief responses following participation in a bereavement group (Malone, 2012). Typically, adolescent girls may be willing to express sadness and fear but are more reluctant to verbalize feelings of anger and aggression, whereas the reverse may be true for adolescent boys.

Given their socialization to externalize distress, adolescent boys may be more prone to act out emotional pain through anger and aggression. Adolescent girls tend to be more openly reactive to loss than boys but are also more receptive to social support, which may make social support a more crucial stress-buffering factor for adolescent girls (Gilligan, 1982; Gore & Eckenrode, 1996). Adolescent boys may be more reluctant than girls to seek out therapy following a loss. However, this may have more to do with the socialized norms and expectations rather than adolescent boys' desire to seek out support through therapy. These gender role related differences in symptom expression and behavioral response often manifest themselves during loss, grief, and trauma-focused psychotherapy. Therapists need to be alert to ways in which grieving and traumatized adolescents express or inhibit their emotional responses based on gender role related expectations and societal, cultural, and familial norms. However, therapists must avoid treating adolescent clients in a gender role stereotypic manner, and be sensitive to how gender-related socialization impacts adolescents.

In terms of grieving patterns or styles, Doka and Martin (2010) have identified two distinct styles of expressing or adapting to a loss, grief, or trauma experience as intuitive or instrumental, which are influenced by gender but not necessarily determined by gender. "These patterns differ in the experience, expression, and adaptation to grief" (Doka & Martin, 2010, p. 125). Many adolescents will present with a blend of these two styles, typically somewhere on a continuum between intuitive and instrumental, but tend to be socialized to conform toward one end or the other.

Intuitive Grieving Style

Adolescent girls are expected as females to exhibit a grieving style toward the intuitive end of the continuum, which includes overtly expressing emotions by crying easily in response to sadness and loss, and readily and willingly sharing their thoughts and feelings with others. An intuitive grieving style involves an outward expression of one's thoughts and feelings about one's loss, grief, and trauma responses and reactions, with particular attention paid to emotional content. Intuitive grievers experience their loss, grief, and trauma events deeply and intensely. This tends to take a toll on their energy level, leaving them emotionally and physically exhausted. "Anguish and tears are almost constant companions" (Doka & Martin, 2010, p. 57). The behaviors that are typically associated with an intuitive grieving style involve (Doka & Martin, 2010, p. 63):

- Feelings are typically experienced very intensely
- Expressions such as crying and lamenting the loss, grief, or trauma experience tend to mirror the adolescent griever's experience of intense inner pain
- Successful adaptive strategies such as going with the feelings facilitate the experience and expression of feelings
- There are often prolonged periods of confusion, inability to concentrate, disorganization, and disorientation due to the enormous amount of energy expended on experiencing and expressing feelings
- Physical exhaustion occurs from intense expressions of feelings like crying or venting anger; this can also produce anxiety due to hyperarousal

Instrumental Grieving Style

Adolescent boys are expected as males to exhibit a grieving style toward the instrumental end of the continuum, which involves a more cognitive than affective approach to loss, grief, and trauma, while keeping emotional content hidden or camouflaged. As a result, they are expected to be more problem focused and use distraction and diversion as coping methods. This tends to take a toll on their capacity to think through situations due to the cognitive energy involved in processing through loss, grief, and trauma. Instrumental grievers may exhibit impaired cognitive activity, confused or fuzzy thinking, disorientation, concerns about concentration, and disorganized thinking (Doka & Martin, 2010, p. 66). The behaviors that are typically associated with an instrumental grieving style involve (Doka & Martin, 2010, p. 85):

- Differentiation between thoughts and feelings, with thinking as the predominant experience to loss, grief, and trauma; feelings have less intensity
- General reluctance to discuss feelings, although they certainly do experience sadness, anxiety, and loneliness
- Mastery and control of oneself and the environment through thinking and planning activities
- Focus is on problem solving as a strategy that enables mastery of feelings and control of the environment, particularly on issues created by an adolescent's loss, grief, and trauma experience
- Brief periods of cognitive dysfunction are common due to the amount of energy invested in intellectual inquiry to understand loss, grief, and trauma experience rather than affect
- Energy levels are enhanced, with a desire to do something, yet symptoms of hyperarousal such as racing heart and shallow breathing go unnoticed

Influences on Grieving Style

"The griever's desire for social support, the need to discuss feelings, and the intensity and scope of activities are varying ways of expressing grief and are often important in distinguishing between patterns" (Doka & Martin, 2010, p. 53). These ways of expressing grief are developed over time and are based on adaptive strategies. Some adolescents have not needed or have had the opportunity to adapt to loss, grief, and trauma over any length of time. This may be their first loss, grief, or trauma experience, and the first time that they, family members, friends, and perhaps even their therapist have learned about their grieving style. Adolescents who have had multiple experiences of loss, grief, and trauma, and especially those beginning in early childhood, have developed a grieving style and adaptive strategies. Gender role socialization is not the only indicator of an adolescent's grieving style. Other factors that shape grieving style include an adolescent's personality, cultural expectations and norms, and familial modeling of emotional regulation in response to loss, grief, and trauma experiences.

CHAPTER 6

What Grieving Adolescents Need

This chapter focuses on what is needed by adolescents struggling with loss, grief, and trauma. This includes consistent contact and connection with and support from the people involved in their lives such as parents and extended family members, friends and peers, teachers and other school personnel, neighbors, other caring adults, and the larger community. It explores the difficulty many adolescents face in talking with people about their loss, grief, and trauma experiences, and the expectations they have of their parents and other adults during this important time. The necessity and desire of time spent with friends and peers will be examined as a healthy component of coping through loss, grief, and trauma. Additionally, the importance and benefits of adolescents receiving appropriate psychoeducation and information about loss, grief, and trauma is explored. Finally, the use of symptom management and reduction techniques is outlined and described as a beneficial component of working with adolescents enduring loss, grief, and trauma experiences.

FAMILY CONNECTION

Support provided by an adolescent's family, whether defined as parents, extended family members or relatives, or other adults in her life, is imperative to an adolescent facing loss, grief, and trauma. She may at times look like she is doing well, and other times she seems to completely fall apart. Parents and other adults may perceive her as being alternately overly dramatic and aloof. This can be confusing to parents, especially if their adolescent is someone who previously handled and managed multiple school tasks and projects as well as a busy social life. Adolescents experience complex and intrusive thoughts and feelings associated with loss, grief, and trauma, which can lead to fear and confusion. This can be particularly true if it is the first time an adolescent is grappling with the impact of loss, grief, and trauma.

The majority of adolescents both need and desire a strong familial support system that involves consistent contact and connection among members. This often surprises parents and other caring adults who may believe that adolescents no longer require or want their involvement given the natural separation and individuation process inherent in adolescence as a developmental phase. Adolescents benefit from being taught positive coping skills from the caring adults in their lives. The hope is that parents and other caring adults have themselves developed appropriate coping skills in response to their own life challenges. Instances of loss, grief, and trauma in adolescents' lives offer the opportunity for adults to provide them with life wisdom and guidance. Adolescents also need to be provided with some healthy distractions such as physical activity and other interests during challenging times. This gives them permission to enjoy a time out from grieving and reassurance that life can still offer good times that include laughter, fun, and silliness. Adolescents need to be able to problem solve and must have this modeled for them as they navigate the fallout from loss, grief, and trauma. They will be able to do so if they are taught the techniques of healthy emotional regulation, for which they need adults in their lives.

Family members such as parents and other caring adults often have great influence on adolescents. They are typically the first modelers of how to handle loss, grief, and trauma experiences. Although separation from parents and forming one's own identity is paramount for and a necessary task of the adolescent years, they still look to their parents in times of challenge, particularly if this involves loss, grief, and trauma. Adolescents can be highly influenced by the comments made by their parents about emotional expression and regulation, often inadvertently seeking approval regarding their actions and behavior. Of course this is contingent on the degree of cohesion or closeness within the family unit, and if parents are currently and have in the past been consistently emotionally available and nurturing to their adolescent. Methods of coping with loss, grief, and trauma are provided by parents via modeling and are dependent on their capacity to respond in positive and healthy ways to stressful life situations. Equally important is parents' ability to adapt to the changing and sometimes challenging needs of their developing adolescent. The problem-solving abilities and affective responsiveness of a family are tested during times of loss, grief, and trauma. When a family evidences a healthy balance of affective involvement with their adolescent, it reinforces the ability of the adolescent to internalize healthy emotional relationships with others. This is a necessary skill for adolescents in communicating effectively about their needs during loss, grief, and trauma experiences.

Consideration must be given to how loss, grief, and trauma is faced and explained within an adolescent's family unit, social setting, and cultural context. Culture influences an adolescent's experience, expectations, and acceptable expressions of loss, grief, and trauma. It is important to explore with adolescents what they have been taught and what they believe about loss, grief, and trauma as well as death and dying. Culture also influences patterns of attachment and defines the meaning of different types of losses, as well as who gets to grieve (Doka & Martin, 2010). Some cultures inform adolescent girls and adolescent boys about how to grieve in gender-specific ways, at times with much rigidity and little variance in these expectations. This can be underscored by familial adherence to cultural norms and expectations regarding gender-specific reactions to loss, grief, and trauma. Yet, some families opt to allow adolescents to respond to loss, grief, and trauma in ways that are more in character with the individual adolescent.

Adolescents can feel discomfort talking with parents about their feelings and are often disappointed in their parents' reactions. Many adolescents expect more support from their parents than they actually receive. Parents are unsure how to react to their adolescent, especially if, for example, the deceased is someone to whom the adolescent was not particularly close. Unfortunately, adolescents are often perceived by family members as resilient and not seriously affected by loss. Adults may not recognize the severity of the loss, grief, or trauma event to the adolescent. An adolescent's perception of lack of parental support in her time of need makes it very difficult to find people she can trust and with whom she can talk about her loss, grief, or trauma experience. Since adolescents have an investment in projecting an image of independence and that they have control over their lives, parents may mistakenly assume that they are not wanted or needed for help with emotional regulation in response to intense situations. Adolescents can certainly look like adults in physique, body development, and attire yet still struggle with the emotional immaturity of their age. Their parents and other adults in their lives may react to this pseudosophistication with unrealistic expectations for emotional control in their responses to loss, grief, and trauma.

FRIENDS AND PEERS

Adolescents highly value their friends and understand the importance of maintaining these relationships. They receive trust, support, loyalty, and empathic understanding from friends during difficult times. With the cognitive changes taking place during adolescence that allow for understanding another's perspective, they have an increased capacity both to be there for one another and to seek out reciprocal support and understanding. This is especially important during the challenging times and emotions that accompany an adolescent's experience of loss, grief, and trauma. Most adolescents tend to seek out their friends and peers when going through a loss, grief, or trauma event, and they may feel most comfortable receiving support from their friendship and peer systems. They want to spend time with friends via physical proximity, phone, text, Skype, and Instagram, and seemingly do not want to be around parents and other family members. Yet simultaneously, they can feel different from and misunderstood by friends and peers. Adolescents may not always know what it is they need and expect from their friends.

Parents can sometimes feel dismayed by the amount of time an adolescent wants to spend with friends, especially if loss, grief, and trauma have impacted the family unit. Parents may want to keep adolescents close to them for their own protection and comfort; however, adolescents need to make sense of these experiences with trusted friends within whom they can safely confide. Being with friends is both a necessity and a healthy component of an adolescent's attempt to cope with loss, grief, and trauma. Not only is time spent with friends used for sharing and making sense of thoughts and feelings that can seem senseless at times, but friends can offer a healthy diversion from the constant pain of loss, grief, and trauma. Adolescents need to be able to act like adolescents, to be in the moment, to laugh and cry with friends and peers, and to realize that their lives will continue in the face of loss, grief, and trauma. As noted by 15 year-old Jess, whose uncle died suddenly from a heart attack and to whom he was quite close, "He was my favorite uncle. We played video games together and he taught me to lift weights." Jess's father was angry that he wanted to be with his friends right after the funeral rather than stay at the house with his family. "I know he was his brother but I needed to get out of there. I didn't want to cry anymore." Jess went to his best friend's house and "Talked about my uncle and laughed about some of the memories. When I teared up Paul just sat with me."

PSYCHOEDUCATION

Loss, grief, and trauma intervention and treatment must incorporate a psychoeducation component of age-appropriate information for adolescents regarding loss, grief, and trauma. This is essential in order to assist adolescents in identifying the physical, social, emotional, and cognitive symptoms they may be experiencing and struggling with related to the loss, grief, or trauma event. Often adolescents do not know or understand their loss, grief, and trauma responses. They may question the normalcy of their responses, wondering if there is something wrong with them if they cannot cry or cry too much or encounter changes in sleep or appetite. The appropriate information benefits them by reducing their perceptions about their reactions or responses as being wrong, abnormal, bizarre, or related to personal shortcomings or faults (Saltzman et al., 2002). This involves teaching adolescents the vocabulary for both expressing their responses to and communicating about loss, grief, and trauma. The dissemination of appropriate information lets adolescents know what to expect in terms of their own reactions as well as the responses of others to both the loss, grief, and trauma experience and to them as individual grievers. It helps to both normalize and validate their experiences, particularly when they learn to identify, normalize, and validate their loss, grief, and trauma responses within physical, social, emotional, and cognitive domains.

Adolescents are typically egocentric, existing in a world that revolves around their needs, wants, desires, thoughts, and feelings. Because of this natural narcissism, they often believe that their loss, grief, and trauma responses are "unique and incomprehensible to both themselves and others" (Hooyman & Kramer, 2006, p. 143). They often do not understand the powerful feelings or the range of emotionality that are connected with these experiences. They must be given permission and the emotional space in which to talk openly about loss, grief, trauma, and death. Explanations must be given that all of their emotional expressions, such as crying and sadness, feelings of intense anger, unfathomable confusion, and an intense guilt, are natural and expected components of a normal grief reaction to loss and trauma. They may feel emotionally assaulted by their own system, especially if these are new experiences for which they have not had the opportunity to learn or employ the ability to regulate their emotions.

Vocabulary of Loss, Grief, and Trauma

Many adolescents do not know where to begin to talk about their loss, grief, and trauma responses. This stems from growing up in a death-denying society where grief and death are rarely discussed in either the home or the community, although they are a very real part of life. Yet loss, death, and the grief that follows are universal experiences that everyone encounters regardless of culture, gender, socioeconomic status, or religion. Often, adults do not want to burden someone so young with thoughts of loss and death, and often tend to leave adolescents out of the decidedly adult conversation about decisions made or responses to loss, grief, and trauma, especially within the family unit. Adults also struggle with how and when to talk about the intense and often confusing and conflicting thoughts and feelings that they themselves experience.

Adolescents need to be taught the vocabulary of loss, grief, and trauma. They benefit from death education that focuses on what happens to the body during and after the dying process, as well as what to expect from grieving rituals. They need to be given permission to express their thoughts and feelings. Some adolescents need to talk about their spiritual and/or religious beliefs, and about what they believe happens after a person dies. Their belief system may or may not align with that of the family. For many adolescents, this becomes their first experience with grappling with these profound and potentially meaningful thoughts or ideas, and giving them the emotional space to talk about them can prove quite beneficial.

Information

Adolescents need to be kept in the informational loop. They need full access to information about the loss, grief, or trauma event. If it is a family member's impending death, then they need to know the specifics about the illness, the processes involved, and the expectations regarding how, when, and where the loved one is going to die. Adolescents also need to know what is expected of them regarding spending time with their dying loved one, in being able to express their thoughts and feelings, and in saying goodbye. "Including adolescents in events, explaining to them what is happening, and reassuring them about their role in the death and in the family are crucial" (Hooyman & Kramer, 2006, p. 149). For many adolescents confronted with the impending death of a loved one, there is a struggle with existential questions about the meaning of life and death as well as the meaning of their own lives. The more reflective and mature an adolescent is, the more this type of questioning is evident. If advance directives are involved, then adolescents need to have these explained to them and to be informed about details related to any decisions made.

If a loved one's death is due to an accident, homicide, or suicide, an adolescent must also be informed of this. Giving her the details must be done in a caring and supportive manner. If she is not given details, then too much is left to her imagination about what occurred and if it could happen to her or others about whom she cares. For months after 17 year-old Stacey's best friend was murdered, she spent hours late at night searching on the Internet for police reports to gain information about the details of the murder and

to keep updated about her friend's murderer. She became
her need to gather information because no one else could g
her questions, which caused her parents great concern. "It k
worrying about it happening to anyone else." Keeping adolesce
helps them begin to adjust and adapt to a world without thei
as well as to the sometimes randomness and oftentimes meaning   ͻ or
loss and trauma events.

SYMPTOM MANAGEMENT AND REDUCTION

Adolescents are often overwhelmed by the inconsistency and intensity of
their emotional range in response to loss, grief, and trauma. Again, they
are going through a normal developmental period of emotional growing
pains and have not yet developed the ability or bandwidth necessary to
recognize and emotionally regulate their responses and reactions. However, once adolescents learn to recognize and acknowledge their physical,
social, emotional, and cognitive responses to loss, grief, and trauma, they
can then be taught to both manage and reduce their symptoms. Therapists can utilize symptom management and reduction techniques with
adolescents during individual, group, or family therapy sessions. Symptom management and reduction can be taught to adolescents as a skill
set to be used at any time, and it is an extremely important component
of loss, grief, and trauma intervention and used in ongoing therapy. The
majority of adolescents welcome learning these very transportable skills
that they can use at home, at school, while they are with friends, and
when they are alone. This very teachable and useful skills set includes
relaxation techniques, breathing retraining, grounding techniques, making an appointment with grief, and increasing awareness of an adolescent's physical reactions and learning to soothe the body.

Relaxation Techniques

The physical loss, grief, and trauma responses of adolescents often take
the form of somatic complaints that include headaches, stomachaches,
and muscle tension that affects the entire body. Adolescents can be taught
a variety of relaxation techniques that help to reduce these symptoms.
One technique that is often employed and easily taught is a graduated
muscle tensing and relaxing. This can be done in either individual or
group therapy settings. The adolescent can do this sitting in a chair or
lying on a sofa in the therapist's office or group room. The preference is
for the adolescent to close her eyes; however, some adolescents are not
comfortable doing this. If that is the case, then she can focus on a specific

spot on the wall or ceiling or focus on an object in the room. The adolescent is instructed to start with her feet, to clench her toes tightly, to hold this tension for a count of five, and then to quickly release or relax the tension. This graduated muscle tensing and relaxing is worked up the body involving all muscle groups, such as legs, arms, stomach, chest, shoulders, face, and head.

A healing light relaxation technique is similar to the graduated muscle tensing and relaxing in that it also employs the entire body. This exercise is particularly beneficial for adolescents who somaticize their thoughts and feelings related to loss, grief, and trauma. This can be done with the adolescent sitting in a chair or lying on a sofa in the therapist's office. Again, the preference is for the adolescent to close his eyes, but if he is uncomfortable doing this, then he can focus on a specific spot on the wall or ceiling or focus on an object in the room. The adolescent is instructed to select a color that represents soothing, healing, and peace to him. He is to imagine this colored light shining warmly on his head and coursing throughout his body as it soothes his brain, his eyes, the optic nerves, his ear canals, and his throat. The therapist guides him through imagining the healing light connecting with his tissues, muscles, tendons, and with each internal organ, working its way down his body to his toes. The therapist is to use a modulated and soothing tone of voice as she guides the adolescent through each of the above relaxation techniques.

Once an adolescent is instructed and guided through how to utilize these methods at home, he can opt to have background music, ideally consisting of soothing and calming tones. Some adolescents have discovered guided relaxation podcasts and have downloaded them to their phone or computer. Others have taped their own voice guiding them through this technique.

Breathing Retraining

Often when adolescents feel anxious and frightened, they tend to engage in shallow breathing. This can cause dizziness, dry mouth, tightness in the throat, pressure in the chest, a racing heart, and tingling in the fingers. These physical sensations contribute to an increase in anxiety and fear, causing some adolescents to worry that they are actually dying. Breathing retraining is a method of taking deep and focused breaths as a calming technique during times when adolescents are disturbed by their thoughts, feelings, and physical reactions. By retraining the way they breathe, adolescents gain an increase in the awareness of when they stop breathing as a maladaptive method to reduce upsetting feelings, or when they are breathing shallowly. Adolescents can be instructed to do this exercise while listening to music with a specific slow rhythm or beat, or to do this in silence. They can close their eyes or create a focal point such as a dot or spot on the wall, or other object. Some adolescents select a picture or image that they hang on their wall at home in order to practice breathing retraining. The adolescent is instructed to breathe in slowly through her nose to a count of six. She is to then exhale slowly through her mouth making a slight wind sound or saying a calming word such as "soothe" to a count of six. After exhaling, she is to count to four and repeat the exercise. The adolescent is encouraged to do this breathing retraining for eight cycles, and to practice it at home two to three times per day. Eventually, she will be able to employ this calming technique in many situations without much thought, as a very natural exercise.

Grounding Techniques

In therapy sessions, some adolescents may become overwhelmed by their thoughts and emotions as they talk or think about their loss, grief, and trauma experiences. They describe a sensation of floating away or not being able to stay present in the room or in the moment. This is the system's way of dissociating or disengaging from thoughts, feelings, or memories that create a trauma or grief overload. When this occurs, grounding techniques can be used to effectively keep the adolescent present. Additionally, the adolescent can be taught to utilize these outside of the therapy office for whenever she experiences this overwhelming reaction. These grounding techniques can be done almost anywhere and are particularly beneficial when an adolescent is alone and feeling flooded by loss, grief, and trauma reactions.

- Instruct the adolescent to focus on sensations. Ask her to listen to the sounds around her. Perhaps she can hear the birds outside, the hum of an air conditioning or heating unit, or the sound machine in the therapist's office. She is to bring each of these background sounds to the foreground and really focus on them, describing in great detail what it is that she hears.
- Have the adolescent describe the temperature and if it is cool or warm on his skin. When he is outdoors, he can do this exercise by focusing on the feel of the sun on his skin and the quality of the light, and if there is a breeze, how it feels on his skin, his face, his hair, his arms, his legs, and on his entire body.
- Ask the adolescent to listen to your voice as you speak to her in modulated, soothing tones. Remind her that she is in the therapy

office, what day it is, the month, and the time. This orients her back to the moment.

- Ask for the adolescent's permission to touch him lightly on the hand as you tell him that he is in the therapy office with you. He can also be instructed to gently rub his hands together or to lightly tap the back of his hand or his knee while regulating his breathing. Do this for a few minutes until you notice him completely present with you in the therapy room.
- An adolescent can be instructed to place one hand on her forehead and the other on the back of her head while regulating her breathing. She can also wrap her arms around herself and gently rock while regulating her breathing. If her eyes are closed, have her open them slowly and gently, looking at her lap, and then have her meet your eyes. State, "You are here. You are here."
- Sometimes lying flat on his back on the floor, especially at home, can ground an adolescent who is overwhelmed and disassociating or disconnecting. He is to feel all the areas where his body touches the floor, taking deep and slow breaths. Have him state, "I am here. I am here."
- Ask the adolescent to look around the therapy office and name three red items in the room, and then name two round objects in the room. Then have her look at the floor, then the ceiling, then at you.

All of these grounding techniques can be integrated with breathing retraining.

Make an Appointment With Grief

This exercise can be modeled in the therapy office as a concentrated and purposeful exercise in focusing on the feelings, thoughts, and memories related to an adolescent's loss, grief, or trauma experience. Although the exercise mentions grief as the focused objective, it can be focused on whatever troubles the adolescent most about his loss, grief, or trauma experience. It can be one specific feeling, memory, or thought. It could be a physical, social, emotional, or cognitive reaction or response to his loss, grief, or trauma experience. The adolescent is to make an appointment with grief. Instead of attempting to stop his thinking, he is to take a good look at it by making the time to allow for the thoughts, the feelings, and the sensations to arise. Instead of trying to push his thoughts and feelings out of awareness, he is instructed to pay attention to what comes to the forefront and to stay in that moment. He is to explore both his thoughts and his feelings and speak them out loud. This can be done as a timed exercise for, say, five or ten minutes. The adolescent can make an appointment with grief at home, setting aside five or ten minutes by using a timer, during which he thinks about his loss, grief, or trauma experience. This way, he can begin to give himself permission to allow for sadness, anger, guilt, confusion, or fear at an appointed and specified amount of time. When thoughts and feelings arise, he can set them aside, noting that he will pay attention to them later rather than suppressing them. This allows him to give himself permission to enjoy the times when he is not thinking about his loss, grief, or trauma experience or responses.

Body Awareness and Body Soothing

When adolescents, like all people, are confronted with loss, grief, and trauma, they typically employ a fight, flight, or freeze response. All of these emotionally based responses land in the body and reside there, being stored up only to arise or become hyperaroused when triggered by thoughts, feelings, or memories related to the adolescent's loss, grief, or trauma experience. This neurobiological linkage causes physiological or body dysregulation when an adolescent is presented with a reminder and thrown back into the somatic experience of her loss, grief, or trauma. Fight, flight, or freeze responses are classified as primitive survival behaviors that emerge when an adolescent feels emotionally vulnerable and is ill equipped to handle the perceived threat. Adolescents who exhibit any of these survival-based fight, flight, or freeze responses are attempting to adapt to a loss, grief, or trauma experience that has overwhelmed them emotionally and dysregulated them physically. To cognitively and emotionally process the loss, grief, and trauma, adolescents must first gain body awareness and learn to body soothe by increasing self-awareness of their overactive and hyperaroused central nervous system.

An important first step is to help adolescents gain awareness of their current body sensations, which "can anchor one in the present, here and now, facilitating separation of past from present" (Rothschild, 2000, p. 107). Helping adolescents become aware of and begin to take control over their physical dysregulation involves teaching them the concept of perceiving their body as an anchor to the moment. Below is an exercise to use in helping adolescents develop body awareness (Rothschild, 2000, pp. 102–103).

- Do not move. Notice the position you are sitting in.
- Pay attention to the sensations you become aware of. Scan your entire body: notice your head, neck, chest, back, stomach, buttocks, legs, feet, arms, hands.

- Are you comfortable? Do not move yet.
- How do you know if you are comfortable or not? Which sensations indicate comfort or discomfort?
- Do you have an urge to change your position? If so, do not do it yet. Just notice the urge.
- Where does that urge come from? If you were to change your position, what part of your body would you move first? Do not do it yet. First follow that urge back to the discomfort that is driving it. Is your neck tense? Is there somewhere in your body that is beginning to become numb? Are your toes cold?
- Now follow the urge and change position. What changes occurred in your body? Do you breathe easier? Is a pain or area of tension relieved? Are you more alert?
- If you have no urge to change your position, you might just be comfortable. Notice the clues your body sends you to signal that you are comfortable. Are your shoulders relaxed? Is your breathing deep? Is your body mostly warm?
- Now change your position whether or not you are comfortable. Do so again if you already changed position earlier. Change where or how you are sitting. Move somewhere else. Try a different chair, stand up, or sit on the floor. Take a new position and hold it. Reevaluate this: Are you comfortable or not? Which body sensations tell you: tension, relaxation, warm, cold, ache, numbness, breathing depth, and location? This time also notice if you are more alert or awake in this position or in the last one.
- Try a third position and evaluate as above.
- Write a few notes about your experience, using the words of body sensation: tension, temperature, breathing.

When hyperaroused and physically dysregulated, an adolescent may become angry, aggressive, and full of rage, with irritability and outbursts of anger where he verbally attacks others. This is an outward or external expression of his grief and trauma, evidenced in a fight response. An adolescent who erupts in anger describes physical symptoms of headaches, body aches and pains, sensations of feeling hot and explosive, with muscle tension poised "To pounce on anyone or anything that gets in my way." Adolescents state that the anger rapidly takes over their entire body, and for many, finding healthy physical ways to discharge the heat and intensity of the anger is beneficial. After adolescents learn to acknowledge that they are hyperaroused and are able to identify their physical sensations as anger, they can then employ strategies to diffuse the anger and calm or regulate the body. Actual physical exercise such as going for a walk, working out at a gym, running, and doing calisthenics at home is useful. Some adolescents discover that learning to relax can control their angry sensations. This is done through slow and intentional breathing techniques as discussed above.

When hyperaroused and physically dysregulated, an adolescent may become sad and depressed, possibly suicidal, and unable or unwilling to talk about her thoughts and feelings. This is a turning inward of her grief and trauma, evidenced by a flight response, an avoidance of the emotional pain. An adolescent who engages in risky behavior such as substance using and abusing, disordered eating, running away, and avoidance of involvement in previous activities or relationships describes physical symptoms of numbing out, dissociating, and an inability to feel her body. "It is as if I don't even exist. Sometimes I can't feel my face or my arms or legs." Adolescents recognize feeling a sense of fear and terror that overwhelms to the point of needing to disconnect by daydreaming, watching Netflix for hours, or playing video or computer games endlessly. After adolescents learn to acknowledge that they are hyperaroused and are able to identify their physical sensations as sadness or fear, they can then employ strategies to diffuse these emotions and anchor or regulate the body. Teaching adolescents grounding techniques as previously outlined is very beneficial to keep them in the moment and able to feel their bodies.

When hyperaroused and physically dysregulated, an adolescent may become lethargic and nonresponsive, have difficulty making decisions, and be unable to take care of herself as she had previously. This is grief and trauma that stops her from engaging in her normal daily life, evidenced by a freeze or collapse response. An adolescent who has difficulty returning to her pre-grief or pre-trauma world describes physical symptoms of a sense of coldness, heaviness in her limbs, intense fatigue, slowed heart rate, shallow breathing, diarrhea, nausea, and an inability to move her body. Adolescents recognize this sense of immobilization as a feeling of defeat and helplessness where they have no control. Helping adolescents to reengage in joyful activities that involve movement and play is beneficial in regaining their physical presence.

Body soothing can take many forms and is dependent on each adolescent's loss, grief, and trauma experience and physical response. Knowing what an adolescent feels physically is the first step to knowing why he feels that way emotionally. Gaining a sense of agency allows adolescents to be in control of their lives. It begins with their awareness of their "subtle sensory, body-based feelings," because the greater their awareness, the greater their potential to control their lives (van der Kolk, 2014, p. 95).

CHAPTER 7

The Use and Impact of Technology and Social Media

Over the past 15 to 20 years, technology and social media have become an increasingly important and expected component of adolescent life, as outlined in Table 7.1. Adolescents are heavy users of electronic communication to include many forms such as cell phones, email, and text messaging (Subrahmanyam & Greenfield, 2008). They have grown up with all aspects of technology both at home and in the classroom, using it socially, recreationally, and educationally, making them digital natives. Most adolescents are at ease with and quite adept at using technology on a daily basis. They constantly blog, watch, tweet, Snapchat, Skype, and post to YouTube, Facebook, and Flickr (Hope & Ryan, 2014). Cell phones can be seen as an extension of an adolescent's hand, in a pocket

Table 7.1 Technology and Social Media (Hope & Ryan, 2014; van Dijck, 2013)

Technology	Year Began
PlayStation	1994
Xbox	2002
MySpace	2003
Skype	2003
Facebook	2004
Flickr	2004
YouTube	2005
Twitter	2006
Wii	2006
Instagram	2012
Snapchat	2013

or purse, or on the table or desk next to them. They rapidly and repeatedly look at and text messages while watching movies, talking to others, doing homework, and so forth. They videotape and post to Facebook on an ongoing basis. They play both solitary and group games on their cell phones, tablets, and other gaming platforms such as Xbox, PlayStation, and Wii (van Dijck, 2013). They simultaneously stream movies on their laptops while doing homework or hanging out with one another.

Constant and immediate technological connection is an important characteristic of adolescent relationships, whether it is with close friends or larger groups. This constant technological contact and connection has become an integral part of the adolescent landscape. The adolescent world is a relational and social one, and they view their use of technology as the tool for social interaction. Given that adolescence is the prime developmental phase for increasing interpersonal interactions and learning about their role in relationships, it is not surprising that their use of technology is extremely popular (Sofka, 2009). This is how many, if not the majority of, adolescents become informed about activities occurring both at and outside of school, since it is the primary mode of communication between groups of adolescents. Many group activities are planned via text messaging, such as setting the time and place for seeing a movie, or whether or not groups of friends are attending a dance, sports, or other school-sponsored event. This is how word spreads and arrangements are made about parties and other events outside of school.

Many adolescents have ready access to computers and other technological devices in the privacy of their bedrooms. This allows them the freedom and independence to connect with anyone at any time. If they cannot sleep, they can text or Skype with a friend who is still awake. If they have a question about homework or a school event, they can receive an immediate response rather than waiting until the next school day. If they feel misunderstood by the adults in their lives, they can reach out to a friend or peer for support and feedback. If they have a loss, grief, or trauma experience, they are most likely to use technology to connect with a friend or peer. If there is no one with whom to connect, then there is the Internet and the multitude of online resources, which can provide a relatively safe way to gain both information and support.

THE USE OF TECHNOLOGY IN GRIEVING AND COPING

The use of technology often plays an important role in the grieving and coping process of adolescents, acting as a lifeline among adolescents, and especially among those who have experienced loss, grief, and trauma. In the immediate moments after a loss, grief, or trauma event, many adolescents turn to one another to find meaning and attempt to make sense of a senseless occurrence. They simply need the validation and confirmation from other adolescents about their reactions and emotions, possibly at the expense of communication with parents or other supportive and concerned adults. In an attempt to gather as much information as possible about an event, adolescents turn to one another to find out not just about the facts of a situation but also about how to react, think, behave, and feel in response to loss, grief, and trauma experiences. Many adolescents are more comfortable with friends and peers than with adults and will depend on these relationships to inform them about grieving and coping norms. They often do not know what to do and seek out those who they would normally turn to for advice regarding other adolescent issues such as dating, school, music, clothing, and activities.

With the advent of smart phones, another type of technology that adolescents use proficiently is videotaping. As 17 year-old Damien shows a video of his ex-girlfriend's funeral after she died in a car accident, "Here is the video of her funeral. Even though she was my ex-girlfriend, she was my first ever girlfriend and I still cared for her. See the doves. They were freed from the cage at the end. It was so sad and so beautiful. She was a beautiful person even if we didn't date any more. My girlfriend now didn't want me to go to the funeral, but I'm glad I went."

The majority of adolescents have immediate access to the Internet, where they can find information about loss, grief, and trauma as well as the possibility of social support. Many adolescents will search for information about the effects of loss, grief, and trauma in an attempt to understand their reactions. If no one else in their circle of friends and peers is going through this, then they will turn to the Internet for guidance and social support. Sofka (1997) refers to adolescents' use of technology in grief-related circumstances as "thanatechnology." They use both the Internet and other resources in the digital world as ways to help them cope with loss, grief, and trauma.

Benefits

The use of technology is very appealing to adolescents, not only because everyone else is using it but also due to the immediacy of connection. Texting and posting on Facebook can provide an immediate response, which can act as a reciprocal exchange of thoughts, ideas, and feelings. This is crucial for adolescents who often guess at what the appropriate or "right" reaction or feeling is to a given situation, especially if it involves loss, grief, and trauma. As noted by 15 year-old Alicia after learning of a classmate's death, "My first reaction was I didn't know what to do. I didn't really talk to him. We weren't really friends. And then I found out that he had died. I didn't know if I was allowed to cry. I didn't cry or anything, I just kind of like sat there." Social norms and values get defined by social media, such as Facebook, where adolescents can immediately turn to their friends and peers to reference their reactions. They constantly post their thoughts, feelings, ideas, and opinions within moments of an event. This is in rapid real time and very immediate.

It is important to understand that adolescents use technology as a way of helping them understand and cope with loss, grief, and trauma. Acceptance of this fact can go a long way in adults' understanding of and connecting with adolescents who use technology on a regular basis, and who may increase their usage during a critical time of loss, grief, and trauma. Parents and other caring adults often misunderstand the need for speed of connection among adolescents, perceiving their immediate texting action as disrespectful, unfeeling, and uncaring. Yet the connection among friends and peers is imperative, normal, and expected, which can offer grieving adolescents some normalcy in an otherwise abnormal situation. For some, the use of the Internet and email can act as a protective effect against depression and chronic grief (Vanderwerker & Prigerson, 2004). This is important information that underscores the need and desire of adolescents to connect to one another and to search for ways to manage their loss, grief, and trauma responses.

Many adolescents utilize the Internet for information regarding health and mental health related issues. They look up the signs and symptoms of depression and anxiety, cancer, and other diseases. They may be fearful that whatever caused the illness or death of a loved one might happen to them. Some adolescents seek answers to questions they have about the grieving process. Unfortunately not all information on the Internet is accurate, up to date, or evidence based. After his father died quite rapidly after the onset of cardiovascular problems, 14 year-old Terrence looked up information about grief on the Internet and stated, "Well, I guess I am in the acceptance stage of grief 'cause I accept the fact that he is dead and not gonna be in my life any more."

Risks

Many adolescents have access to telephones, cell phones, email, and instant/text messaging. Technology has created avenues through which information travels rapidly and in real time, where information about a loss, grief, or trauma event can travel rapidly from one adolescent social network to another. Their use of technology creates unlimited access to friends, support systems, and information (James, Oltjenbruns, & Whiting, 2008). As the news spreads quickly with potentially few buffering effects, adolescent loss, grief, and trauma responses can be both profound and intense. If adolescents learn of a classmate or peer's death due to suicide, there is the additional risk of a contagion response, raising the possibility of suicide attempts among adolescents (Hanson, Tiberius, Hodges, Mackay, McNaughton, Dickens, & Regehr, 2002). At the very least, this news is upsetting and extremely sad to any adolescent who learns of this devastating loss. Given that the majority of adolescent deaths are sudden and unexpected, adolescents are emotionally unprepared to hear about the unforeseen loss of a classmate or peer. Although the impact of receiving this news can vary from individual to individual, adolescents typically do not have a framework of experience in which to place the immediate news of a sudden death.

The negative aspect of this constant contact is that rumors are spread rapidly, which can have dire consequences for some adolescents. It is akin to the old-fashioned game of telephone, where one person whispers a sentence to another, which is then whispered to another, and so on until it reaches the last person in a circle. The resultant end message is quite distorted, often not even resembling the original sentence. Given that text messages can be directly read, the message can still become enhanced, distorted, added to, deleted from, and changed drastically from the original. This can be especially true when an adolescent hears about a loss, grief, or trauma event via text or phone, or even on Facebook.

Jennie, a 16 year-old, describes how she learned about her cousin's death from cancer, "In class another cousin sent me a text that said don't take this hard, try to take it easy. She started out kidding around with me so I didn't know if she (cousin) died. Then I started to cry. It was really hard. She was only 15. And then I got a call afterward from my aunt who told me." This occurred on a normal school day without any chance of forewarning or the possibility of a caring adult preparing Jennie for sad and painful news in a private setting. She was left to deal with her loss and grief alone until she could connect with family members. Another adolescent, 16 year-old Andrea, learned of her estranged mother's death via Facebook. They had just reconnected without the knowledge of her father, which left Andrea without a supportive network when she saw her half-sister's Facebook post that their mother had died "At 2:45 in the morning. What was I supposed to do? I wasn't going to get to talk to her

Table 7.2 How Girls Learned About Peer's Death

Number of Girls	How Girls Learned About Peer's Death
6	Text message during school
6	School announcement
5	Family member face-to-face
4	Another student face-to-face during school
3	Witnessed
3	Call on cell phone during school
1	MySpace during school

anymore. I wasn't going to get to tell her like everything that's going on. I was just getting to know her and what she was like. Now that's gone."

In a study that explored the impact of peer death on adolescent girls, it was determined that the majority of them learned about the death via social media and while at school (Malone, 2010). Of the 28 peer deaths reported, there were six instances of the information being received via text message during the school day. Regarding another six instances of peer death, this information was announced by the school principal over the intercom at the end of the school day. There were four instances of girls hearing about a peer's death face-to-face from another student while at school. The news of three deaths was obtained via cell phone calls during the school day, and one learned of her peer's death over MySpace, also while at school (see Table 7.2).

These notifications occurred with no buffering effects of warning, taking an adolescent aside to discuss the tragedy with them privately, or providing a calm and quiet environment for them to begin to process the loss and grieve.

CONTINUING BONDS

The concept of continuing bonds was initially proposed by Klass, Silverman, and Nickman (1996), who view it as a healthy and normative response to the death of a significant person and as a way of maintaining an ongoing relationship with the deceased person. "Maintaining a tie with a deceased loved one can be self-affirming and comforting, and the maintenance of the bond can be more freeing than its denial" (Moss, 2004, p. 77). Adolescents by their very nature are tasked with the separation individuation process, which involves identity formation by both integrating and rejecting aspects of others. The death loss of someone who had meaning to the adolescent can be interpreted as losing a part of oneself. Therefore, "to affirm the deceased other can affirm the self"

(Moss, 2004, p. 78). Death does not necessarily sever the relationship with the deceased but transforms it as continuing bonds, which entails keeping the deceased person as an ongoing presence in an adolescent's life. An adolescent may have imaginary conversations or thoughts about what the deceased person would say or do in a given situation or want to share an aspect of her day with the deceased person. This can be especially beneficial when she experiences a significant event such as the beginning of a new relationship or a romantic breakup, and hitting milestones such as obtaining a driver's license, landing that first job, preparing for and attending prom, high school graduation, and acceptance to college. As do all people, adolescents like to share these experiences with friends and family members. The death of a significant person leaves a void in an adolescent's life. That person's absence is definitely noticeable during these pivotal life events, which further underscores the importance and necessity of adolescents becoming aware of and informed about the concept of continuing bonds as an ongoing relationship or attachment.

There are tasks involved during the process of grieving, both non-death and death loss as well as trauma. Worden and Winokuer (2011) describe a model that incorporates four tasks that inherently relate well to adolescent development and include a continuing bonds component. The tasks are (Worden & Winokuer, 2011, pp. 58–65):

1. To acknowledge the reality of the loss. This task requires adolescents to both believe and to not believe, or deny, that the loss or trauma has occurred. There may be searching behavior, as evidenced by 16 year-old Jennie's statement after the death of her 18 year-old sister due to a car accident, "I keep going to her bedroom to ask her for help with math, and then I almost get there and remember that she's not gonna be there." The ongoing nature of the relationship that Jennie will continue to have with her deceased sister is based on the understanding and acceptance that her sister is indeed no longer physically present in her life. Even after acknowledging the reality of losing her sister to death, she will continue to have a bond with her through memories, reminiscing, and maintaining emotional connection.

2. To process the pain of grief. This task requires adolescents to allow themselves to have feelings in response to loss and trauma rather than deny or avoid their emotions through distracting activities. After the death of his father, 15 year-old Derek became very focused on his schoolwork, achieving high grades and

receiving praise from his teachers. However, he quit the baseball team because, "I don't have time to play. I don't have time to be sad or anything. Grades mean everything, and I need to get home to my mother and little sis. They need me now." On the surface it appears as though Derek has stepped up to become the man of the house; however, he remains distracted from his feelings by his self-imposed responsibilities. He is acting stoically as many adolescents do in the face of loss, which is intended to hide or camouflage his feelings, yet it is important for him to identify, acknowledge, and express them in order to process the pain of grief.

3. To adjust to the world without the deceased. This task requires adolescents to adapt to the ensuing changes that occur in their lives after a loss or trauma experience. It is crucial to help adolescents as they adjust to multiple levels and layers of change that can happen over time. Bettina, 17 years old, had an extremely close relationship to her grandmother who raised her. Together they weathered Hurricane Katrina in New Orleans and made their way to Texas. However, her grandmother had health problems and died approximately four months later. Bettina endured "layers and layers of loss" with a deep and unrelenting sadness as she needed to adapt and adjust to more change in her life.

4. To find an enduring connection with the deceased in the midst of embarking on a new life. This task requires adolescents to develop and maintain continuing bonds with the deceased in a way that allows them to move forward in their lives. They need to be able to take the deceased loved ones into the future and hold them in the present while simultaneously remembering them in the past. After 18 year-old Tomas's mother died from a prolonged illness when he was 14 years old, he talked about taking her with him to college: "I have a picture of her that I sometimes talk to. She's going with me to college 'cause I know she would be so happy to see me there and to hear all about my classes and friends." As he moves forward into young adulthood, Tomas may draw considerable and beneficial strength from the continuing bond that he maintains with his deceased mother by using her viewpoint to make decisions, and identifying what she would have wanted for him.

Developing, maintaining, and restructuring continuing bonds relationships with a deceased loved one benefits adolescents as they strive, and sometimes struggle, to adapt to loss, grief, and trauma in healthy ways.

FACEBOOK AS A VIRTUAL GRAVE MARKER

Given that a person's Facebook page can exist well beyond the person's death, it can be viewed as a virtual grave marker. Some adolescents continue to visit the page, with some posting comments on the deceased person's wall, thereby creating an electronic memorial. Pictures are posted and memories are shared among groups of adolescent mourners. Kasket (2012) looked at "in-memory-of" groups on Facebook, and found themes that pertain to the experience of continuing bonds. These include "comfort of communication," where adolescents post messages sharing everyday experiences such as what occurred in school that day, or who won the football game. Adolescents are often a disenfranchised group of mourners, left out because they are not family members or perhaps a close friend of the deceased; however, social networking grants them admission. These sites offer a community of support and understanding, which is beneficial to adolescents processing a loss, grief, or trauma event. Because of the immediacy of this connection, adolescents can continue to post messages to honor, commemorate, and continue a bond with the deceased.

Facebook pages have morphed into Facebook memorials or virtual memorials, which have become a significant part of our culture's death and dying rituals (Jones, 2004; Sofka, 2009). They are often utilized or visited by adolescents as a way to make sense of the death of a loved one and to reconnect to the deceased (DeGroot, 2012). Adolescents grieve online and maintain the continuing bond with the deceased by writing something to the deceased. There is immediacy of contact and connection, which aligns with an adolescent's impulsive nature and tendency to live in the moment. Facebook pages can be accessed any time of the day or night and from any location, whether it is from the adolescent's bedroom, classroom, or walking in the school hallway. This constant availability is imperative to adolescents. As noted by Joseph, age 16, whose friend and fellow trumpet player died suddenly in a car accident, "Sometimes I just really miss him, especially right after band practice, so I go to his Facebook page and see stuff he posted like photos and such. And maybe I'll tell him about practice or that we lost the football game on Friday." This aspect of continuing bonds through his friend's Facebook page can offer solace in times of loneliness and allow for remembering and reminiscing.

Many adolescents are reluctant to show strong emotions connected to loss, grief, and trauma, which makes posting on a Facebook memorial page less risky emotionally. Facebook memorials allow grieving adolescents to maintain the bond, to preserve their relationship with the deceased (Roberts, 2004). An aspect that is central and characteristic of being an adolescent is living in a relational world, which makes ongoing communication with the deceased a healthy component of the grieving process. Visiting and writing on Facebook memorial pages offers relational continuity to adolescents. Their visits and posts typically increase on anniversaries, birthdays, and holidays. Adolescents often post things that remind them of the deceased, such as song lyrics or poetry both from popular culture and those they have written for the deceased. Others will post pictures of themselves as if the deceased can view them. As noted by 17 year-old Cassandra, whose young aunt died of kidney disease, "We used to love to shop together so I took some selfies in this new skirt and showed her. She would've loved it!"

The nature of interactions online allow for more self-disclosure by adolescents. It may be more emotionally safe than other types of interaction, particularly as compared to face-to-face connection. Adolescents can express their innermost and true thoughts and feelings without the fear of being judged, dismissed, rejected, or belittled. They cannot be told what to feel and how to feel it, or be placated in any way. Some of their posts may contain memories of times together with the deceased, similar to an instant replay of the events. Friendships are often cemented with "remember when . . ." stories, and posting these on the deceased's Facebook page continues that bond. There is also the opportunity to say goodbye, which is particularly important if the cause of death was sudden and unexpected, which is unfortunately often regarding adolescent deaths. Adolescents get to say things they regret not getting to say to the deceased, to express their thoughts and feelings in a safe and enfranchising way. As noted by 17 year-old Malcolm regarding the sudden death of his ex-girlfriend due to a car accident, "She was my ex-girlfriend and since I had a new one, I couldn't really talk to her any more. I never got to tell her that I still cared about her, and I wished we could be friends." Malcolm described how beautiful it was when the doves released at her funeral flew away, "Beautiful like her," and that he posted the video on her Facebook page.

Some adolescents' posts are made up of events from day-to-day life as a way to include the deceased. They include updates and announcements about relationships and events as a way to include the deceased in high school life. Many adolescents post about things they see and do that remind them of the deceased. As noted by 16 year-old Josh, whose younger sister died by suicide, "The wildflowers are blooming and I think of you when I see the blue ones at the end of our street." There is also communication about promises made and kept. Josh posts to his sister, "I kept the promise made at your funeral. I try to laugh every day and check in with Mom. She's doing okay." Other adolescents make requests to the deceased to watch over the living and believe this happens. As noted by 15 year-old Marinda, whose older brother was killed by rival gang members, "I know you're watchin' over me. I'm tryin' to do good." Adolescents "often attempt to renegotiate their identities by continuing or maintaining bonds with the deceased, as people generally do not forget their friends just because they are dead" (DeGroot, 2012, p. 204).

Continued access to Facebook pages of the deceased acts as a way of enfranchising adolescents and their loss, grief, and trauma experiences. It is also interesting to note that adolescents take the concept of continuing bonds with them beyond Facebook. Many have pictures of their deceased loved ones on their phones, tablets, and laptops. Some create their own photo collages of the deceased, places they frequented, and things they enjoyed. As noted by 16 year-old Jason, whose twin sister died in a scuba diving accident, "She liked Hello Kitty so now I have this ongoing photo collection on my phone for every time I see one." Jason pulls out his phone and scrolls to a photo collage of Hello Kitty items such as slippers, a coffee mug, a clock, and a cake designed as Hello Kitty. He also posted these pictures on her Facebook page as a way to continue his bond with her.

Kasket (2012) summarizes the reasons that people, particularly adolescent digital natives, use Facebook as a modern-day medium of continuing bonds with the deceased. There is the comfort of communication with no judgmental or demeaning responses from others, including adults and peers. They get to experience the vividness of their deceased loved one's telepresence in the form of photos, posts written by the deceased, and any other virtual memorabilia on the deceased's page. It offers adolescents the opportunity to embrace the importance of making an investment in order to maintain a continuing bond with their deceased loved one. Technology is an inherent and normal aspect of an adolescent's world, and using it to visit or post on a deceased loved one's Facebook page becomes part of their normal everyday activity. Most importantly, the fear of the bond breaking is the main motivating factor for adolescents' continued connection. This can be especially poignant as adolescence is a transformative developmental phase that includes adaptation to rapid change. The consistent ability to connect and continue a bond, whether with the deceased or the living, is paramount.

CHAPTER 8

Group Therapy: An Ideal Modality

Group therapy as a modality of intervention for adolescents has histori-cally been utilized for a wide variety of issues and concerns that have an impact on this population (Gitterman & Shulman, 2005; Malekoff, 2004). Some of these groups have focused on topics such as substance use and abuse, substance use prevention, bullying and victimization, teen pregnancy, interpersonal skills development, life skills development, health and wellness, nonlethal self-injury, parental divorce survival, stress reduction and relaxation techniques, test anxiety, and for coping with various mental and physical health issues. Groups can provide a frame-work for adolescents toward understanding the impact of loss, grief, and trauma in their lives, and an opportunity to effectively build support, mutuality, and connection among group members (Balk, 1996; Gitter-man & Shulman, 2005). There is a positive connection between social support and the adjustment of adolescents, which is understandable given the importance of peer relationships in the development of cogni-tive and social skills during adolescence (Tedeschi, 1996). This makes group therapy especially significant since loss, grief, and trauma can be an isolating, private experience for many adolescents (Lattanzi-Licht, 1996). This suggests the need for and importance of developing and providing groups in various settings that focus on reducing loss, grief, and trauma responses experienced by adolescents during a time of vulnerability and intense emotions.

Groups are an important and intrinsic component of an adoles-cent's life, which makes participation in a group an effective treatment modality for adolescents confronting loss, grief, and trauma (Aronson, 2004). Adolescents are naturally part of many groups, such as their high school grade and their various classes. These represent both small and large groups that often intersect in hallways between classes as social groupings. Adolescents who participate in band, orchestra, theater, and choir belong to groups. Those who are on athletic or academic teams are also members of groups. Many adolescents seek out and find specific groups to join, both formal and informal, as well as within the school setting and the wider community. Adults often ask adolescents about which group or groups they belong to, curious about their involvement in the larger school community.

Participation in group therapy acts as a protective factor for adolescents coping with loss, grief, and trauma experiences. It can enhance healthy functioning and resiliency, and normalize and validate their thoughts, feelings, and behavior. The following outlines some important strengths-based group practice principles adapted from Malekoff (2004).

- Form groups based on adolescents' felt needs and wants, not just their diagnoses
- Structure adolescent groups to welcome the whole person, not just the troubled parts
- Integrate both verbal and nonverbal activities
- Decentralize authority and turn control of the group over to the adolescents
- Maintain a dual focus on individual change and group process
- Understand and respect group development as a key to promoting change in adolescents

Group therapy can often be viewed as an ideal modality for adolescents to confront and work through loss, grief, and trauma issues. It can provide an environment that promotes resilience, which acts as a protective factor against the physical, social, emotional, and cognitive aspects of adolescent loss, grief, and trauma responses. "Groups of peers struggling together buffer life's blows and can even turn adversity into opportunity" (Lee & Swenson, 2005, p. 587). There are themes that emerge when adolescents gather together to discuss their feelings, thoughts, and behaviors as they relate to loss, grief, and trauma experiences. Recognition and acknowledgment of these common themes help to both normalize and validate them for adolescents who may be judging themselves as abnormal, crazy, or weird due to their loss, grief, and trauma responses. Adolescents who are part of cohesive friendship groups and social networks that are designed to increase positive connection, personal and collective strengths, and competence, and who exhibit high self-esteem, are likely to face loss, grief, and trauma experiences with fewer long-lasting negative effects (Bearman & Moody, 2004; Steese et al., 2006). The quality of the connection with others contributes to adolescents' psychological health, self-image, relationships, and overall well-being. Many participants in bereavement support groups report more freedom in expressing feelings, and that they are more in control of their lives and are more confident, happy, and able to connect to others (Tedeschi, 1996). This is especially important for adolescents since they can often feel set apart, different from peers, and as if they have no control over their lives due to loss, grief, and trauma. Support groups have been shown to reduce both physiological and psychological stress and are noted to be the single most consistent predictor of improved adjustment to loss, grief, and trauma (Goodkin, Baldewicz, Blaney, Asthana, Kumar, Shapshak, Leeds, Burkhalter, Rigg, Tyll, Cohen, & Zheng, 2001).

In a review of the efficacy of bereavement interventions, it is noted that adolescents show more improvement in depression and conduct following group participation after experiencing the death of a parent (Schut, Stroebe, van den Bout, & Terheggen, 2001). There are profound effects on adolescent survivors of deaths that result from diseases and accidents or intentionally inflicted death due to homicide, suicide, or interpersonal violence (Hill & Foster, 1996). Clinical literature and grief and loss studies both suggest that group modalities are the preferred treatment for adolescents. This illustrates the healing power afforded adolescents through group work focused on loss, grief, and trauma.

Groups for adolescents designed to meet their needs around loss, grief, and trauma are typically either school-based groups or provided in private therapy practice offices. They can be gender specific or coed, of mixed age, or age and grade specific. The pros, cons, benefits, and challenges of providing groups in these contexts will be discussed. The progression in cognitive development, sense of mastery, competence, and control makes adolescents amenable to group participation. "Group work and the dialectical processes it promotes to advance mutual aid provide an ideal context for accommodating and fostering this quantum leap in cognitive development during adolescence" (Malekoff, 2004, p. 8).

There is an abundance of literature on the efficacy and principles that surround group work (Cohen, 1995; Drumm, 2006; O'Conner, 2002; Shulman, 2006). Clinical literature endorses group therapy as the treatment of choice for adolescents for these reasons: (1) adolescents more readily accept feedback from peers than from adults, (2) groups promote peer interactions and emphasize the importance of relationships, (3) group norms have a socializing impact, (4) group participants benefit from the work done by other group members, and (5) groups allow for the opportunity to simply listen without having to respond (Glodich & Allen, 1998; Malekoff, 2004; Oltjenbruns, 1996).

The effectiveness of adolescent groups can be measured by how each group, regardless of focus or context, acts as a protective factor to mitigate against risk. "Protective factors are conditions that buffer young people from the negative consequences of exposure to risk by either reducing the impact of the risk or changing the way a person responds to risk" (Hawkins, 1995, p. 14). Risk factors may include poor coping skills and a nonexistent or ineffective support system (Corr & Balk, 1996). Adolescent groups provide an environment that allows for the growth-enhancing impact of protective factors to occur as well as the creation of resiliency (Lee & Swenson, 2005; Malekoff, 2004). Protective factors within a group modality include the normalization and validation provided by other adolescent group members as they share their stories and experiences of loss, grief, and trauma. The group acts as a context for social reinforcement, which can improve adolescents' adaptive and social skills and reduce self-destructive behaviors (Masten, Best, & Garmezy, 1991; Rittner & Smyth, 1999). Although group members are typically not forced to talk and share thoughts and feelings, the group process itself provides a forum of curiosity where adolescents want to know one another and want to be known by one another. Self-examination and "cognitive restructuring occur with peer support and reinforcement which enables adolescents to cope more effectively with the emotional, familial, and social stressors in their lives" (Rittner & Smyth, 1999, p. 71). Adolescent group members give and receive feedback, which provides an opportunity for self-examination and reflection. The group process goes beyond the time adolescents spend in group, as they take with them what they have learned about themselves in relating to other adolescent group members.

A comparison between group and individual therapy for adolescents via a meta-analysis of nine studies yields results supporting group treatment as more effective with adolescents (Tillitski, 1990). Again, this underscores the power of normalization and validation that group participation provides to adolescents coping and struggling with the impact of loss, grief, and trauma. Interventions with grieving adolescents have included both support groups and self-help groups (Pennebaker, Zech, &

Rime, 2001; Pesek, 2002; Schut et al., 2001; Schuurman, 2008; Stevenson, 2008; Stroebe & Schut, 2001; Tedeschi, 1996; Valentine, 1996), as well as school-wide postvention groups (Catone & Schatz, 1991; Hill & Foster, 1996; Komar, 1994; Rickgarn, 1987; Rickgarn, 1996; Stevenson, 2002). Summarily, groups for adolescents have been historically utilized to offer support and skills building as they navigate through loss, grief, and trauma.

COED VS. GENDER-SPECIFIC GROUPS

There are cogent arguments both for and against coed or gender-specific groups as well as for diversity or specificity regarding age and grade. Additionally, when developing groups for adolescents struggling with loss, grief, and trauma, there is the question of whether or not adolescents would relate more closely with someone who has had the same loss, grief, and trauma experience. In other words, decisions need to be made about the group's homogeneity or heterogeneity. Regardless of differences, the physical, social, emotional, and cognitive responses are the same, making this the point of intersection and recognition among adolescent group members.

Coed Adolescent Groups

Coed adolescent groups allow for the development of interpersonal skills with both same and opposite genders. One positive feature includes the fact, with the exception of all-girls and all-boys schools, that high schools are composed of both males and females. This includes teachers, coaches, principals, and other school personnel. The world is peopled with both genders. Another positive feature of coed adolescent groups focused on loss, grief, and trauma as that they get to see that responses are not necessarily gender based or gender specific. Both males and females cry. Both females and males get angry. Loss, grief, and trauma experiences increase both male adolescents' and female adolescents' vulnerability to depression, anxiety, and other potentially damaging responses, and both benefit from the support and understanding offered by group participation. Coed groups allow both males and females to witness one another's ability to be vulnerable in discussing their loss, grief, and trauma responses as well as the universality of these responses. Chapman (2003) surveyed 469 high school adolescents, 58% females and 42% males, regarding the importance of five social supports during loss and grief experiences. Both male and female adolescents benefit equally from receiving peer support, teacher support, neighborhood support, parental support, and general social support during times of loss and grief. The similar need evidenced by both genders is a good argument for providing coed groups for adolescents coping and struggling with loss, grief, and trauma experiences.

Adolescent Girls' Groups

The advantage to gender-specific groups for adolescent girls has to do with how girls are socialized to "lose their voices" when in the company of males (Brown & Gilligan, 1992; Gilligan, 1982). In coed groups, girls will allow boys to interrupt them more often than they will girls in all-girls groups. Girls are socialized to be emotionally expressive but can become silenced in the company of boys. Some of this is based on the traditional female role, which instructs her to please males, not compete with males, act inferior to males intellectually, restrict her personal ambitions, be silent, accommodate the needs of others, be dependent on males, and enhance her status through association with males (Choate, 2014). This equation is not present in all-girls groups.

Adolescent girls experience having their voices, thoughts, and feelings heard more readily in gender-specific groups. Adolescent girl groups typically focus on putting words to the feelings surrounding loss, grief, and trauma. They learn to tease out the tangled emotions of guilt, shame, anger, and sadness rather than identifying and labeling all as sadness. In times of stress, girls are socialized toward an affiliative "tend and befriend" response, which typically creates a very supportive environment in adolescent girl groups (Rose & Rudolph, 2006).

Adolescent Boys' Groups

Late adolescent boys may benefit from participation in coed groups, whereas early adolescent boys can benefit from gender-specific groups (Way, 2011). This is related to the friendship needs of these ages, as discussed in chapter five on adolescent boy relationships. Boys in early adolescence are more apt to explore and discuss their emotional responses to loss, grief, and trauma in an all-boys group. They more readily trust one another during this time in their development. As they grow into late adolescence, many boys are more comfortable discussing their emotional selves with females, with the exception of those boys who develop a best or close friend. They become more cautious exposing their feelings to other boys. Some of this may be related to our culture's instillation of homophobic fears in adolescent boys. Additionally, in times of stress boys are socialized toward an aggressive "fight or flight" response, which may create an adversarial or at least uncomfortable and emotionally unsafe environment in adolescent boy groups (Rose & Rudolph, 2006). Some of this may be averted or avoided when adolescent boy groups are led by a male therapist who can appropriately model beneficial ways of discussing emotionally vulnerable thoughts and feelings related to loss, grief, and trauma experiences.

GROUPS IN VARIOUS SETTINGS

Groups for adolescents are provided in a variety of settings to include high schools, private therapy practice offices, and community settings such as churches and recreation centers. Adolescent groups are also held in psychiatric and medical hospitals as inpatient and intensive outpatient groups. Basically, wherever there are adolescents, a group can be formed. However, most groups focused on loss, grief, and trauma are typically held in the school setting or in private therapy practice offices.

Groups in School Settings

Schools have long been the setting for groups, since adolescents spend the majority of their daily lives at school. It is the logical place to offer adolescent groups, since "without emotional and social well being, academic progress will slow or stall altogether" (Ziffer, Crawford, & Penney-Wietor, 2007, p. 155). Adolescents perform better in school when they learn healthy and functional ways to manage and cope with their loss, grief, and trauma responses. Research supports the effectiveness of groups and group interventions in the schools, particularly if they are "both short in session length and overall time," which makes them a realistic endeavor (Gerrity & DeLucia-Waack, 2007, p. 104). Groups focused on loss, grief, and trauma responses are designed to teach adolescents the skills to function beyond these experiences. They also provide an emotionally safe and supportive environment in which to discuss their thoughts and feelings related to their loss, grief, and trauma experiences.

It is more adaptive and more convenient to incorporate groups into the weekly school schedule than to schedule groups in locations that involve transportation arrangements. This may ensure attendance and participation. Additionally, many adolescents are involved in extracurricular activities that meet before or after the school day. Given such a busy after-school schedule, this may create a barrier to adolescents attending a loss, grief, and trauma group outside of the school setting.

However, there are some disadvantages to groups held in the school setting. Group therapists cannot guarantee anonymity for adolescent participants, although group rules typically include maintaining the confidentiality of who is involved and what is discussed. Adolescents may be concerned about being judged by others who know of their group participation, such as teachers, administrators, school counselors, and of course their classmates and peers. Due to this vulnerability, open discussion and sharing of thoughts, feelings, and behaviors related to loss, grief, and trauma experiences may be deterred and perceived as emotionally unsafe.

Groups can provide a structured outlet in the school setting, especially for adolescents struggling to maintain focus in the classroom due to loss, grief, and trauma responses. Group participation allows for connection with peers, who often have similar and universal experiences. This is especially true if adolescents have experienced the death of a friend, peer, or teacher within the school community (Saltzman, Steinberg, Layne, Aisenberg, & Pynoos, 2001). Groups can provide an emotionally safe place for adolescents to share their fears, frustrations, and joys with others who may understand them better than the adults around them. Groups in the school setting also share a common community culture, neighborhood culture, and school culture, with understood and accepted norms and values specific to behavior related to loss, grief, and trauma. These community-accepted norms and values also dictate how adolescents are expected to grieve. (The exception to this is private schools that may draw students from various neighborhoods rather than the immediate and surrounding neighborhood.) Yet these within-school communities operate as a microcosm with similarly shared norms and values.

There are four main types of groups that are typically held in school settings: working or task groups, psychoeducational groups, counseling groups, and psychotherapy groups (Paisley & Milsom, 2007). The type of group offered to adolescents is dependent on the group's purpose, composition, and topic. School-based groups have been provided to focus on a myriad of topics to include improving academic success (Webb & Brigman, 2007), diversity sensitivity training (Nikels, Mims, & Mims, 2007), adolescents of deployed soldiers (Rush & Akos, 2007), adolescents with incarcerated parents (Lopez & Bhat, 2007), parental separation and divorce (Ziffer et al., 2007), and adolescents with disabilities (McEachern & Kenny, 2007). Other topics for groups have historically included eating disorders, anger management/bullying, pregnancy prevention, social skills/competency, substance abuse prevention, as well as loss and grief. Many of these have incorporated classroom interventions (Gerrity & DeLucia-Waack, 2007). Some of these also include homework to be completed outside of school. In summary, there are many opportunities and needs for adolescent groups in the school setting.

Groups in Private Therapy Practice Offices

Many therapists in private therapy practice offices offer adolescent groups that cover a range of purposes and topics. Some of these parallel those offered in school settings such as groups developed to focus on eating disorders, parental divorce/separation, social skills development, and substance abuse prevention/recovery. Groups in private therapy practice offices are also provided for adolescents struggling with a specific diagnosis such as anorexia/bulimia, ADD/ADHD, or major depressive disorder. Other private therapy practice offices may offer a gender-specific group such as a group developed for high school girls struggling with social skills, depression, anxiety, and nonlethal self-injury. Another example might be a group provided to increase social skills for adolescent boys who have been diagnosed on the autism spectrum.

An advantage to providing adolescent groups in private therapy practice offices is the ability to hold groups composed of adolescents from different high schools. This ensures confidentiality and anonymity for group members. It also adds to heterogeneity, in that adolescents do not belong to the same school community and most likely do not live in the same neighborhood. With the variety of high schools represented by group membership, there is also the advantage of increased diversity in ethnicity, race, and socioeconomic status. The heterogeneous nature of these groups helps to normalize, validate, and universalize adolescents' loss, grief, and trauma responses. They meet other adolescents from differing schools and backgrounds struggling with the same thoughts, feelings, and behavior.

Disadvantages or barriers to adolescents participating in groups held in private therapy practice offices may include the out-of-pocket cost of private therapy and the need to transport adolescents from school to the private therapy practice office. Depending on adolescents' extracurricular activities, they may not have availability in their schedule to participate in a group outside of school hours. Increased traffic in some areas can become a barrier to joining a group for some adolescents. One private practice therapist described how her adolescent groups represented schools from her city as well as five adjacent or suburban areas. However, over time, with an influx of residents and the resultant increase in traffic, many parents were no longer able to get their adolescents to the group on time and without driving for more hours than was desirable. These disadvantages can cause barriers to some adolescents participating in groups outside of the school community.

GROUP ACTIVITIES

The inclusion of group activities helps adolescents to coalesce as well as take ownership of their group. A beneficial and beginning activity to incorporate in groups with adolescents is the handing out of a blank journal and instructing them that it is for them to use as a tool for exploring feelings about loss, grief, and trauma. It is there for when they feel sad, angry, frustrated, guilty, or alone, and is available in the middle of the night or throughout the day. It is to be written in a talking method rather than as a diary about the events of the day. The group therapist can instruct adolescents to use it in a more structured format by giving prompts to provide a concrete method of processing emotions. It can be used in an unstructured format for adolescents to explore thoughts, feelings, questions, concerns, conflicts, problems, solutions, and as an ongoing communication or relationship with their deceased person.

It is very important to begin first groups with activities that help adolescents get to know one another. Below are some activity ideas to employ in the group setting, beginning with icebreakers and evolving into deeper and more meaningful content.

Icebreakers

Groups that begin with nonintrusive icebreakers of typically playful activities allow individual group members to get to know one another in emotionally safe ways. Icebreakers also foster the trust necessary for adolescents to share their very personal experiences of loss, grief, and trauma. To encourage and set the stage for active participation, a "getting to know you" activity involves the group sitting in a circle and tossing a small ball, pillow, or any other object to one another. As each person catches it, they say their name. Keep this going and add other categories such as their school grade, favorite movie, favorite book, favorite activity, or where they would travel if given the choice.

Another icebreaker involves instructing adolescents to get creative with their names. An example of this:

Sad
Energetic
Ravenous
Ended
Nervous
Artistic

Serena is a particularly artistically gifted adolescent, successfully managing an eating disorder, and working through the recent death of her father. This is a fun and potentially revealing activity that acts as a creative prelude to further written or verbal exploration of an adolescent's thoughts and feelings. It offers both creative flexibility and structure (Moss, 2012).

Stress Relievers/Coping Strategies
This is a group activity whose objective is to expand on practical ideas for dealing and coping with stress in the lives of adolescents. Using a large piece of paper or poster board, group members are to list the things they do to de-stress. They are instructed to add anything to the list that helps them relax or shut down their thinking, calms them physically, and quiets or regulates their emotions. Typical list items might include listening to music, playing an instrument, sleeping, taking a walk, talking with a friend, drawing, painting, shooting hoops, swimming, playing a video game, playing with the cat or dog, or watching a movie. This can be an ongoing list where adolescents add to it as they discover additional effective stress-relieving or coping strategies.

Telling the Story
Group therapy developed for adolescents who are working through the death of a loved one needs to include a focused activity on telling the story. This can be accomplished as a written or verbal activity but can only occur after adolescents have coalesced and connected as a group and feel some semblance of safety in being emotionally vulnerable. The objective is to encourage adolescents to focus on the circumstances of their person's death and how it has affected them. This activity is designed to provide an opportunity for adolescents to reflect on their loss, grief, and trauma experience. Questions and prompts include:

- Who died? Tell us how he or she died
- When did your person die?

- Tell us how you found out about it
- Where were you and who were you with?
- Describe your immediate reaction
- Did you see your person after his or her death?
- Explain how you feel now
- Share a memory about your person who died

Much can be learned about an adolescent from her verbal and nonverbal responses to these questions and prompts. Additionally, paying attention to other adolescent group members' responses and reactions to the adolescent's telling of her story can provide invaluable information about each adolescent's own loss, grief, and trauma experience.

Affirmations

This activity involves introducing the concept of affirmations to the adolescent group. They are to come up with some affirmations and write them on a large poster board that is then hung up in the group room. Over time, these can be added to as adolescents discover other positive and helpful affirmations. Some examples:

- It takes courage to feel the pain of grief and move through it
- I will grieve with purpose
- I am not alone
- I will survive
- I find healthy ways to express my feelings
- I am allowed to laugh and to cry
- I need to let other people support me in my grief
- It is alright to take breaks from my grief and do fun things
- There will be hard times and good times

The objective of this group activity is that in thinking about and listing positive affirmations, adolescent group members will begin to achieve a balance by changing some of their self-defeating and negative thoughts to more positive ones.

Supports in My Life

This activity is done individually by each adolescent but then shared aloud with the group. The group therapist creates a worksheet in two columns. The first column has the following listed:

- People who care about me

- Interests that are important to me
- Things that are important to me
- People to add to my list to strengthen my network

Each adolescent is instructed to fill in the second column with responses to the first column. The objective is to help adolescents identify their supports and decide if there are times when they need more support, and to whom they can turn. This also normalizes for adolescents that everyone needs supportive people in their lives.

Helpful and Hurtful Words

This group activity gives adolescents a chance to explore their frustration and other strong feelings as a result of what people have said to them in response to their loss, grief, and trauma experiences. The group reenacts these by creating and role-playing an alternative script. Some things adolescents have been told:

- "But he died last year already. Aren't you over it?"
- "Now you're the man of the house"
- "You weren't really all that close to her anymore"
- "You didn't even like him"
- "What did you expect? He was in a gang"

This activity provides support and encouragement for adolescents to have continued conversations with family members and friends about the words they use. This can be quite empowering and enfranchising for adolescents who typically feel they have no control over what people say to them. They may not be successful in changing what people say, but they are able to give voice to their responses and reactions even if they only do so within the safety or confines of the group environment. This may give them the courage to use a more powerful voice outside of the group.

Group Journaling and Drawing

This activity is a group effort in doing a combination of journaling and drawing. Again, a large poster board is required for this group project or activity. The group therapist selects a few questions, statements, or prompts that align with the issues and themes derived from the adolescents' personal experiences of loss, grief, and trauma. These emerge from the telling of each adolescent's story of loss, grief, and trauma. The questions, statements, or prompts are typed on a sheet of paper and passed around the group. The adolescents sit on the floor with the poster board and materials such as gel pens and markers, and are instructed to select the questions, statements, or prompts that capture their interest or speak to them on some level, and then write or draw them. In this way, they create a group journal or drawing.

One adolescent group composed of six girls, a very close friendship group, met to work through their combined loss, grief, and trauma experience of a seventh friend being murdered. As they worked on their group journal/drawing, the themes that emerged related directly to their loss. Some of the statements or prompts from their telling of their loss story were, "Hatred," "How could this happen?" "She was so young," "Who's next?" "No one talks about her any more, like she doesn't even exist," and "She won't be at the prom." One girl drew a picture of a very fancy and sexy pink dress that their friend planned on buying for the prom. Another girl drew a picture of a monkey with its hands over its mouth and wrote, "Don't talk about it," explaining that no one at school or in the neighborhood would talk about the murder. Another drawing was a very artistic rendering of their friend's face. They then cut out pictures of food from magazines because their friend liked to cook for them. They wrote the names of the characters of their friend's favorite soap opera.

The objective of this group activity is to explore the group's thoughts, feelings, and beliefs about what happened and what the future might hold. For this particular group, it was about a future that does not include the seventh friend, but one that still involves planning for and attending the prom, preparing and eating food, and the continuous nature of soap operas.

Benefit Finding

This group activity involves making another list together. The adolescents are instructed to consider what things in their lives have changed due to their loss, grief, and trauma experience. The group therapist acknowledges that there are most certainly very difficult components to loss, grief, and trauma, yet there can be positive aspects too. Creating a checklist of positive outcomes is a method of benefit finding and making meaning of a meaningless experience. Adolescents might add the following:

- I have a deeper appreciation for life
- I feel closer to the people I love
- I focus on more important things
- I listen to music with meaningful words

The adolescents continue to add to the list until they have exhausted all positive outcomes of their loss, grief, and trauma experiences and responses, and explored all areas of personal growth.

When group activities yield individual drawings or lists, it can be beneficial to allow adolescents to take these objects home to their parents and other caretakers. This sharing of their loss, grief, and trauma work acts as a linkage between the safe environment of the group and the world in which the adolescent lives. It also helps to inform their caring adults about what actually occurs in the group.

CHAPTER 9

The Adolescent Grief and Loss (AGL) Group

The Adolescent Grief and Loss (AGL) group offers a potentially effective and healing setting specifically designed to strengthen connection to others; decrease physical, social, emotional, and cognitive responses; and improve the psychological health of adolescents who have experienced loss, grief, and trauma. It also provides a framework for understanding the effects of these experiences on adolescents.

The AGL group is intended to be both a means and a context for helping bereaved adolescents improve their functioning by meeting their psychosocial needs for learning and applying coping skills, assisting with behavior and emotion, and supporting one another around issues of loss, grief, and trauma. Group intervention has long been viewed as the treatment of choice for many adolescents (Malekoff, 2004), which underscores the importance of providing an effective and evidence-based intervention by therapists in order to enhance individual functioning of grieving adolescents.

INTERACTIONAL GROUPS

Interactional groups are based on the premise that change or therapeutic growth is a complex process that occurs through an interplay of curative or "therapeutic factors" (Yalom & Leszcz, 2005). Table 9.1 summarizes the 11 therapeutic factors and describes how they operate as an interdependent and dynamic process within groups, particularly as they relate to adolescents (Yalom & Leszcz, 2005).

In a study to determine adolescents' perception of therapeutic, or curative, factors in group psychotherapy, Corder, Whiteside, and Haizlip (1981) asked 16 adolescents, ranging in age from 13 to 17 years, from four therapy groups in different clinical settings to rate the most helpful of the 11 therapeutic factors. The adolescents were given 60 cards containing statements

Table 9.1   Therapeutic Factors (Yalom & Leszcz, 2005)

Therapeutic Factor	Description
Instillation and maintenance of hope	This factor derives from positive expectations that people have upon entering group. The instillation and maintenance of hope is based on the belief and confidence in the efficacy of the group format. Hope is required to keep an adolescent in the group until other therapeutic factors take effect.
Universality	This factor brings relief as adolescents realize they share similar experiences, thoughts, and feelings with others. Even though there are differences, adolescents in groups begin to perceive their similarities to one another. In a group, finding out that they are not alone can be a powerful source of comfort.
Imparting information	This is a role taken on typically by the group therapist, although it can also be shared with adolescent group members, who give advice, suggestions, and direct guidance. People in general fear the unknown. Increasing knowledge can decrease fear. Advice given by adolescent group members may be important not so much for the content of the advice, but simply because it is given. This signifies that the adolescent giving it is interested and cares.
Altruism	This can be very powerful for adolescent group members. It offers adolescents the opportunity to be of benefit to others by encouraging them to shift between the roles of help receivers and help providers. Giving to others can be a boost to self-esteem.
Family reenactment (also known as the corrective recapitulation of the primary family group)	The group resembles family in many aspects. Adolescent members will interact with one another as they have interacted with siblings or parents. What is important is that conflicts are not just relived, but they are relived in a positive manner that is functional. The group provides an arena for new behaviors to be tested.
Development of socializing techniques	This factor allows for the development of basic social skills, which can be implicit and indirect or explicitly directed. The group mode is an ideal setting for adolescents to both learn and practice specific social skills. Role-play may be used to enhance social skills.
Imitative behavior	This factor encourages adolescent group members to learn by watching one another tackle problems and situations. This can be a vicarious method of learning new and beneficial behaviors.

(*Continued*)

Therapeutic Factor	Description
Interpersonal learning	This factor is based on the assumption that adolescents develop personalities as a result of their significant interactions in life. Given time, each adolescent group member will begin to be more authentic and will interact with the group members as they act in everyday life. Adolescents do not necessarily need to explain their problems. They will eventually show their true colors.
Group cohesiveness	This is "the group therapy analogue to relationship in individual therapy" (Yalom & Leszcz, 2005, p. 53). It is evident in the degree of engagement and alliance that is formed by adolescent group members. It creates conditions for self-disclosure, interpersonal testing, and exploration to occur. When cohesiveness is present, adolescent group members mean enough to each other to bear the discomfort of working through conflicts. Without cohesiveness, the rest of the therapeutic factors will not have as much, if any, impact.
Catharsis	This factor involves the expression of strong emotions, which is linked with finding meaning in adolescents' life experiences. It must always be accompanied by other factors, as in the process of a corrective emotional experience.
Existential factors	This factor consists primarily of five items: 1. Recognizing that life is at times unfair. 2. Recognizing that ultimately there is no escape from some of life's pain and from death. 3. Recognizing that no matter how close one gets to people, one must still face life alone. 4. Facing the basic issues of one's life and death, and thus living one's life more honestly and being less caught up in trivialities. 5. Learning that one must take ultimate responsibility for the way one lives one's life no matter how much guidance and support one gets from others. This category has been rated by members of successful groups as a very important component for their group experience.

Table 9.2   Therapeutic Factors Ranked the Highest (Corder et al., 1981)

Therapeutic Factor	Item Statement
Catharsis	Being able to say what was bothering me instead of holding it in. Learning how to express my feelings.
Existential factors	Learning that I must take ultimate responsibility for the way I live my life, no matter how much guidance and support I get from others.
Interpersonal learning	Other members honestly telling me what they think of me. The group's giving me an opportunity to learn to approach others.
Family reenactment (also known as the corrective recapitulation of the primary family group)	Being in the group was, in a sense, like being in a big family, only this time, a more accepting and understanding family.

that corresponded with each therapeutic factor, and were directed to put them into the following seven categories: most helpful to me in the group, extremely helpful, very helpful, helpful, barely helpful, less helpful, and least helpful (Corder et al., 1981). The adolescents' responses were then compared to the four therapeutic factors discerned as most helpful by adults, which were *catharsis, interpersonal learning*, and *existential factors*. Adults placed more importance on *catharsis*, whereas adolescents included *family reenactment* as a helpful factor (Corder et al., 1981). Table 9.2 outlines the four factors ranked the highest by adolescents.

The results of this study indicate that groups focused on adolescents need to incorporate assistance from and confrontation by peers, explore new ways of dealing with real-life situations and developing new skills in relating to others, and provide an environment where adolescents feel less isolated (Corder et al., 1981). The use of techniques or tasks that actively structure and provide opportunities for the previously mentioned concepts included as components of the therapeutic factors may enhance growth and movement toward change in adolescent groups (Corder et al., 1981).

MUTUAL AID GROUPS

Mutual aid groups effectively build support, mutuality, and connection among members (Gitterman & Shulman, 2005). A group can be viewed as a system where there is reciprocity between the individual and society. "Essentially, when we lend our strength to others, we strengthen ourselves" (Gitterman, 2004; Gitterman & Shulman, 2005; Shulman,

Table 9.3   Mutual Aid Group Processes (Gitterman & Shulman, 2005)

Process	Description
Sharing data	Adolescent group members provide one another with ideas, information, and resources they have found beneficial. Adolescents can exchange ideas about what has and has not worked for them in the past regarding a particular challenge or problem.
The dialectical process	The group encourages debate between two adolescents, or two subgroups, where there are opposing views. This process emerges from the adolescents' needs to express and resolve an apparent division between adolescent members or subgroups.
Entering taboo areas	This allows adolescents to discuss difficult subjects with the support and encouragement of the group therapist. The permission to enter a taboo area may then invite other adolescents to add their own impressions of the topic or issue.
The "all-in-the-same-boat" phenomenon	This can be a healing process as adolescents learn that others may share similar experiences, feelings, thoughts, and behaviors.
Mutual support	This process enables adolescents to provide one another with empathy and understanding. In small groups, receiving the support of peers can be even more powerful than the support of the group therapist.
Mutual demand	The change process requires mutual demand, which involves adolescents helping one another through specific issues. For example, an adolescent may be expected to take some action and report back to the group the following week.
Individual problem solving	Adolescent group members help another adolescent with a specific problem, which can actually benefit the group as a whole. Usually a connection can be made between an individual adolescent's specific problem and the purpose of the group.
Rehearsal	This is a form of role-play in the group. It involves practicing a task within the group setting while receiving support, advice, and feedback from adolescent group members.
The strength in numbers phenomenon	This allows adolescent groups to work as a unit by taking steps to change together. Individual adolescent members may feel powerless to deal with overwhelming tasks. For example, a group of sexual abuse survivors participated in a "take back the night" march.

1985/86; Shulman, 1999). Mutual aid groups promote resiliency and self-esteem through processes that involve secure and supportive attachments as well as opportunities for the successful accomplishment of tasks (Lee & Swenson, 2005). Table 9.3 summarizes the nine mutual aid group processes as they relate to adolescents.

ADOLESCENT GRIEF AND LOSS (AGL) GROUP MODEL

The goals of the Adolescent Grief and Loss (AGL) group for adolescents who have experienced loss, grief, and trauma are to reduce or lessen physical, social, emotional, and cognitive grief responses and to foster mutual support and connection to others. To that end, the integration of interactional therapeutic factors (Yalom & Leszcz, 2005) and mutual aid processes (Gitterman & Shulman, 2005) define the framework for the AGL group model.

The following examples illustrate how these two theories of group therapy together inform the AGL group, and are described further in the sections on the AGL group structure, stages, and individual tasks as well as their implications. As the adolescents meet to participate in the AGL group, they are given a journal and are instructed to write, draw, and/or jot down thoughts and ideas on a weekly basis about their experiences of loss, grief, and trauma. They bring their journals with them to each of the six AGL groups with the possibility of sharing their content. The therapeutic factor of *universality* and the similar mutual aid group process of the *"all-in-the-same-boat phenomenon"* are at work here as adolescents share the content of their journals, and the group therapist models how to make connections between the similarity of their experiences and ensuing thoughts, feelings, and behaviors, both positive and negative.

Another example involves the fifth of the six AGL group sessions. During the fourth group session, the adolescents are instructed to create a ritual to remember and honor what was lost as a result of their loss, grief, and trauma experience. They also think about any unfinished business and write a letter about what was lost or forever changed. The fifth group session entails the showing and/or performing of the adolescents' rituals as well as the reading aloud of their letters. The therapeutic factor of *catharsis* is involved. It allows for the expression of strong emotions, which is linked with finding meaning in their loss, grief, and trauma experiences. *Mutual support* enables the adolescents to provide one another with empathy and understanding as they read their letters. Receiving support from each other can be more powerful than support from the group therapist.

The integration of these theoretical group concepts applies to the focus of creating an environment of mutual support and growth through the interplay of factors and processes.

THERAPEUTIC FACTORS

The 11 interactional therapeutic factors are incorporated and emphasized in the AGL group as outlined below.

- The *instillation and maintenance of hope* can be a powerful force in groups, particularly as bereaved adolescents see one another learn to cope with their loss, grief, and trauma experience. This therapeutic factor can actually begin prior to attendance of the first group, when potential group participants meet with the therapist.
- *Universality* plays a role in group therapy with adolescents as they learn that others may have some of the same negative thoughts, feelings, and behaviors they do, and that they all share a similar experience of loss, grief, and trauma.
- *Imparting information* includes both didactic instruction and direct advice on the part of the group therapist, specifically around the individual tasks of each of the group sessions as well as the nature of loss, grief, and trauma.
- *Altruism* requires the adolescent to shift between two roles within the group: that of help receiver and help provider. This therapeutic factor benefits the naturally narcissistic adolescent, both allowing and requiring adolescents to step outside of themselves and their own loss, grief, and trauma responses in order to be of benefit to other group members. Adolescents may also be more open to the suggestions, support, reassurance, and insight of their group peers.
- A group often resembles a family within which numerous roles may be played out. *The corrective recapitulation of the primary family group (also known as family reenactment)* allows the adolescents to act as a family within the group, which provides an arena for new behaviors to be tested and relived correctively.
- "*Social learning* is a therapeutic factor operating in all therapy groups" (Yalom & Leszcz, 2005, p. 16). Adolescents benefit from the social network of a group as it normalizes their loss, grief, and trauma reactions within a context of making connections with one another.
- The therapeutic factor of *imitative behavior* occurs when adolescents model supportive behavior. This can be particularly potent as they focus on their shared experiences of loss, grief, and trauma.

- People need acceptance by and interaction with others. *Interpersonal learning* allows for positive and reciprocal bonds to form between the group members. The adolescents learn to communicate with one another, build trust, and share honestly as well as develop relatedness and attachment to one another via their exchanges regarding loss, grief, and trauma.
- *Group cohesiveness* occurs as the adolescents attain some comfort in the group and gain a sense of belonging; "they value the group and in turn feel that they are valued, accepted, and supported" by other adolescents in the group (Yalom & Leszcz, 2005, p. 55). The AGL group becomes their group, their emotionally safe place to confront issues of loss, grief, and trauma.
- *Catharsis* enables adolescents to express emotions, grieve, and find meaning in their losses within the context of the group. "In groups of clients dealing with loss, researchers found that expression of positive affect was associated with positive outcomes" (Yalom & Leszcz, 2005, p. 90).
- *Existential factors* are confronted as the adolescents recognize that life is at times unfair and unjust, as shown by the untimely death of a loved one or the loss accrued by trauma. Mortality issues become evident in adolescents as they experience loss, grief, and trauma.

MUTUAL AID PROCESSES

The mutual aid processes incorporated and emphasized in the AGL group are outlined below. *The strength in numbers phenomenon* is the only mutual aid process that is not included, due to the fact that the AGL group is not constructed to empower group members to confront an agency or institution to make change.

- In *sharing data* adolescents exchange ideas and offer suggestions to one another about what they find helpful in coping with loss, grief, and trauma.
- *The dialectical process* is evidenced by opposing thoughts, feelings, or ideas as presented by two different adolescents or two subgroups. This enables the adolescents to struggle with diverse expressions regarding loss, grief, and trauma as well as to find common ground.
- *Entering taboo areas* may involve discussions of any perceived extreme or negative emotions or thoughts the adolescents may have in response to their loss, grief, or trauma experience. As the

adolescents hear one another express their feelings and thoughts, as well as possible negative or self-destructive behavior, the discussion gives way to an allowed openness about such feelings that may have been viewed as taboo. This may be especially evident if their loss, grief, or trauma experience involved stigmatizing events such as rape, homicide, or suicide.

- "The mutual experiencing of ideas and emotions leads to yet another powerful mutual aid process: the *'all-in-the-same-boat phenomenon.'* This is the healing process that occurs when one realizes that one is not alone and that others share the same problems, the feeling, the doubts, and all the rest" (Gitterman & Shulman, 2005, p. 23). Adolescents who have experienced loss, grief, or trauma can be greatly relieved when they learn that other adolescents have had the same experience, possibly accompanied by some of the same thoughts, feelings, and behaviors.
- *Mutual support* is another mutual aid process observed among the adolescents as they provide empathic support for one another through a difficult time of loss, grief, or trauma. They find they are not alone, that other group members can share their feelings with them. This mutuality can be very powerful in its healing potential among adolescents.
- *Mutual demand* occurs when adolescents in the group confront one another about their thoughts, feelings, and behaviors. This process is beneficial because the adolescents can receive the demand to work since it is being provided by those who have also experienced loss, grief, or trauma.
- The mutual aid process of *individual problem solving* occurs when an adolescent identifies an issue he needs help with and other group members offer possible solutions from their own experiences. This can benefit the group as a whole since most of the adolescents can make a connection between their own areas of need and those of the other group members.
- This can lead to the mutual aid process of *rehearsal*, where adolescents may role-play to help one another find appropriate words and actions to express thoughts and feelings about loss, grief, and trauma.

Many people experience an intense need to assign meaning to a loss, grief, or trauma event, and the relational aspect of the AGL group model benefits adolescents regarding this need (Petersen, Bull, Propst, Dettinger, & Detwiler, 2005). According to Armour (2003, p. 521), "a supportive and accepting audience for meaning reconstruction" is critical for adolescents to make sense of their loss, grief, and trauma experience and to place it within a new life framework. The various creative tasks involved in the AGL group act as a mechanism to elicit and direct meaning making for adolescents. Assisting adolescents in expressing their emotions through physical activities, play, art, and music leads to healthy and successful coping with bereavement (Rask et al., 2002). The use of activities provides a method for "getting things going" (Gitterman & Shulman, 2005) within the group in a nonthreatening way for the sharing of thoughts and feelings.

The AGL group has proven effective in reducing physical, social, emotional, and cognitive responses to loss, grief, and trauma, and the implementation of this group in high schools, community agencies, and clinical settings benefits both adolescents and those who care for them.

THE ADOLESCENT GRIEF AND LOSS (AGL) GROUP STRUCTURE

This section outlines the structure of the Adolescent Grief and Loss (AGL) group as utilized to address the issues surrounding adolescent experiences in response to loss, grief, and trauma. This six-week group can be held in either the school setting or in a therapist's private practice office. Each AGL group session lasts 60 minutes and can be lead by one therapist or co-facilitated by two. It is important to create and ensure a holding environment to contain issues of power and control, especially in the initial phase of the group (Aronson, 2004; Yalom, 1970).

The AGL group is constructed to focus on three main phases: "Creating and Relating," "Coping," and "Transitioning." A full description of the AGL group structure as well as implications of the individual tasks can be found in Table 9.5. Each group begins with a check-in for each adolescent to give a brief description about how she is doing at that moment. Flexibility must be incorporated into each group to allow for the necessary unfolding of each group session. Continuous assessment and monitoring of risks and protective factors as presented through language, materials, and behavior is an important facet of the AGL group model. The group therapist assesses for depression and other mental health concerns on an ongoing basis.

The first phase, "Creating and Relating," focuses on developing a safe environment in which the adolescents can relate to one another in their own voices, narrative language, and expressive manners. This parallels the preaffiliation stage of group development (Garland, Jones, & Kolodny, 1973) and that of "forming" (Tuckman, 1965), where the group is oriented to its purpose and the group members are introduced. Group sessions one and two make up this phase, which fosters the development of positive connection among group members as they express their relationship with their deceased loved one via creative endeavors to include journaling, poetry, drawing, photo collage, and/or music. The focus is on the creative activity of meaning making, which offers adolescents an opportunity to look at their loss, grief, and trauma experiences in a new and unique way (Goodman, 2002; Neimeyer & Jordan, 2002; Petersen et al., 2005). Davis (2001) suggests that finding meaning is a critical step toward adjustment to and making sense of loss, grief, and trauma. Each adolescent shares some of his or her material with the group, and this sharing occurs during each group session throughout the six-week period. Expressive materials such as various sized paper, colored pencils, and crayons are provided by the group therapist to be utilized by the adolescents during group. A journal is provided to each adolescent to use on a daily basis. The adolescents are instructed to journal daily, to track in three columns their thoughts, emotions, and what they feel in their body. The journal can also be used to draw or write in, and is brought to each group session. The journal entries are shared with the group whenever an adolescent wishes to do so. The group sessions end with adolescents given a task to complete and bring to the following group.

The second phase, "Coping," focuses on normalizing the adolescents' thoughts, feelings, and behaviors related to loss, grief, and trauma. Again, the expression of thoughts and feelings is encouraged through the use of various mediums introduced during the first phase. Psychoeducational information is provided to the adolescents about the grieving process and what it entails. The cognitive style of each adolescent is assessed by how they describe their thought processes, feelings, and actions. Various coping strategies are introduced to include the continuation of journaling, the use of physical exercise and body movement, and cognitive restructuring by adding positive cognitions to replace or alter negative thought patterns (Fleming & Robinson, 2001). Additionally, relaxation techniques and grounding exercises are explained and explored. Group sessions three and four compose this phase, which parallels the group developmental stages of both power and control, and the intimacy stages of group development (Garland et al., 1973) as well as those of "storming and norming" (Tuckman, 1965). Judgments may be made of past experiences and behaviors related to their loss, grief, and trauma experiences. Conflict often emerges as adolescents jockey for position by making suggestions or giving advice (Yalom & Leszcz, 2005). Conflict evolves into cohesion as intimacy and trust are established among the adolescents, enabling them to share their coping strategies, thoughts, feelings, and behaviors in response to their loss, grief, and trauma experiences.

The third and final phase, "Transitioning," focuses on acquisition of the necessary skills to continue through life having experienced loss, grief, and trauma as well as without a deceased loved one. This phase parallels the group development stages of differentiation and separation (Garland et al., 1973), as well as "performing and adjourning" (Tuckman, 1965). Protective factors are identified and maximized, such as gaining the ability to regulate and minimize negative grief-related emotions and behaviors, and to instigate and enhance positive emotions (Bonanno, 2001). Often, there is a continuation of group cohesion as adolescents further explore issues of intimacy and trust by sharing their work around the use of ritual as it relates to their loss, grief, and trauma experiences (Doka, 2002; 2008). This phase includes group sessions five and six, and concludes with validation of work done, emotions expressed, and feelings stated.

Table 9.4 outlines comparisons among the AGL group, the typical group development stages of preaffiliation, power and control, intimacy, differentiation, and separation (Garland et al., 1973), as well as the group stages of forming, storming, norming, performing, and adjourning (Tuckman, 1965). Group dynamic forces operate in all groups regardless of their time limitations or whether they are closed or open-ended (Yalom & Leszcz, 2005). Additionally, all groups go through these developmental stages regardless of their purpose or focus.

Table 9.5 outlines the AGL group structure, which describes what occurs in each group session as well as the individual tasks that adolescents

Table 9.4 Comparison of Group Stages

AGL Group	Typical Stages of Group Development (Garland et al., 1973)	Tuckman's Group Stages (1965)	Group Themes
Group Sessions 1 and 2: Creating and Relating	Preaffiliation	Forming	Orientation, introduction, participation, search for meaning, dependency, and sharing of experiences
Group Sessions 3 and 4: Coping	Power & Control Intimacy	Storming Norming	Conflict, dominance, and rebellion, followed by group cohesion
Group Sessions 5 and 6: Transitioning	Differentiation Separation	Performing Adjourning	Continuation of group cohesion, review and validation of work, and celebration

Table 9.5   Adolescent Grief and Loss (AGL) Group Structure

Group Session	Group Description	Individual Tasks
Group Session 1: Creating and Relating	Introductions are made. Norms are established regarding confidentiality, attendance, and members' rights. Each adolescent describes his loss, grief, or trauma experience and talks about what has been the hardest for him. All feelings are normalized and validated, with an explanation that many feelings can be cycled through and revisited in a short period of time. The tone is set for openly using language about death and dying, loss, grief, and trauma.	Each adolescent is to create something that reminds him of what he lost in his experience: write, draw, or make a collage or music playlist. They are to keep journals about their thoughts and feelings about their loss, grief, and trauma experiences.
Group Session 2: Creating and Relating	The items brought by the adolescents are shared and described, read, touched, and/or listened to. The adolescents talk about their loss, grief, and trauma experiences and what they mean to them. The group therapist models empathy and compassion, both verbally and nonverbally. The adolescents are given the opportunity to read from their journals if they wish. The group therapist acknowledges the effort involved in writing about any sadness and/or other emotions the adolescents are feeling. Feedback is given from group members about how they relate to and resonate with what each has written. All expressed feelings are normalized and validated.	The adolescents are instructed to use a Breath Work exercise that involves resting quietly on their beds or on the floor; thinking about their loss, grief, and trauma experiences; and consciously inhaling and exhaling with long breaths. Each adolescent is to keep a Body Awareness Log in their journal, noting any sensations, feelings, or thoughts they experience regarding their body.
Group Session 3: Coping	The adolescents share what they thought and felt while doing the Breath Work exercise. Each of the adolescents shares her Body Awareness Log. The group therapist validates and normalizes any physical sensations described, explaining this as the body's way of grieving and trying to make sense of loss, grief, and trauma. Themes and commonalities are noticed and discussed. The group therapist checks for any difficulty with or resistance to doing the exercise.	Each adolescent is to create a Comfort and Coping Strategies List in her journal that includes what works and does not work for her thus far in getting through, moving on, and coping on a daily basis since her loss, grief, or trauma experience.

(Continued)

Table 9.5 (Continued)

Group Session	Group Description	Individual Tasks
Group Session 4: Coping	The adolescents share their Comfort and Coping Strategies Lists. Group members give feedback and can ask questions about why something works. The group therapist points out themes and commonalities among the lists. The group therapist provides the adolescents with materials to work together as a group in constructing a Comfort and Coping Collage as a compilation of their Comfort and Coping Strategies Lists to be hung up on the group room wall. The group therapist encourages each adolescent's efforts.	Each adolescent is to create a ritual to remember and honor what he lost through his loss, grief, or trauma experience. They are also to think about any unfinished business and write a letter to any lost part of their lives or deceased person(s).
Group Session 5: Transitioning	The adolescents explain and show or perform their rituals. The group therapist suggests ways to incorporate the practice of ritual in everyday life as well as at special or difficult times. Each adolescent reads her letter out loud. The group therapist gives support and encouragement around any unfinished business expressed. All emotions expressed are validated and normalized.	The adolescents are to think about one another and write notes telling what they appreciate about each other as a Validation Activity. They are also asked to summarize what they have learned about themselves while participating in this group.
Group Session 6: Transitioning	During the Validation Activity, adolescents read aloud the notes they have written about each group member. The group therapist supports and encourages this exchange. During the final group, the group therapist summarizes the group's progress and highlights each individual adolescent's growth. Each adolescent verbally summarizes his perspective on his own growth and discusses how he will generalize the coping skills he has learned to other areas of his life.	

are asked to complete prior to the next group (Malone, 2007). As mentioned previously, the group therapist is to maintain flexibility rather than adhere strictly to the group format, which allows for the unfolding of each group session as necessitated by the group participants.

Group therapists must keep in mind that each group constellation has its own personality, characteristics, and dynamics. Table 9.6 further describes the implications of and rationale for each of the individual group session tasks.

The Adolescent Grief and Loss (AGL) group offers numerous benefits to adolescents in that it helps to diminish or reduce physical, social, emotional, and cognitive loss, grief, and trauma responses. Given that many

Table 9.6   Implications of Individual Tasks

Group Session 1	The creation of something that reminds adolescents of their loss, grief, and trauma experience is an attempt at meaning making. It represents how they are organizing their loss, grief, and trauma cognitively and emotionally. The various materials and images used in a collage, for instance, are a demonstration of how the adolescents incorporate their loss, grief, and trauma experience into their worldview of loss. Music has great significance throughout adolescence (Shaller & Smith, 2002). Journaling is a wonderful method for getting inside the thoughts and feelings of adolescents. They write about anything that comes to mind, particularly around loss, grief, and trauma. This gives the group therapist and other group members added insight into the cognitive and emotional processes of each adolescent.
Group Session 2	The Breath Work exercise enables adolescents to control anxiety, fear, and sadness with deep breathing. There will be anxiety-inducing situations in the future, and learning to breathe through the emotions will benefit adolescents in controlling their panic. The Body Awareness Log acts as a somatic barometer of physical well-being. Some adolescents experience aches and pains, headaches, stomachaches, facial and jaw tension, fist clenching, labored breathing, joint stiffness, heart palpitations, and a general malaise (Balk, 1996).
Group Session 3	The Comfort and Coping Strategies List allows the adolescents to reflect on what has been working effectively for them to cope with their loss, grief and trauma, and on what has promise for working for them in the future (Stroebe & Schut, 1999). This in effect empowers adolescents to take care of themselves.

(Continued)

Table 9.6 (Continued)

Group Session 4	Creating the Comfort and Coping Strategies Collage from each adolescent's list bonds the group members further and creates an environment of collegiality that diminishes the sense of loneliness and isolation some may be experiencing. Rituals can be very healing and "can provide a way to master cycles of disruption while remembering, integrating, and transforming the loss" (Dane, 2004). Rituals can provide comfort. Adolescents often face Unfinished Business with their loss, grief, and trauma. This can be dealt with via writing a letter, which is a method that allows adolescents to say the unsaid words, to talk about what they wished they did not say, and to say some final words.
Group Session 5	The Validation Activity provides an opening for adolescents to discuss the difficulty and importance of telling people they care about what they mean to them (Kandt, 1994). Summarizing what they have learned about themselves allows adolescents the time to reflect on their own growth and the possible ongoing change process they are undergoing.
Group Session 6	The final group session incorporates an exercise where everyone looks closely at the gains that have been made throughout the six weeks. The group looks at where they have been, how far they have come, and ahead to the future.

adolescents are considered disenfranchised grievers due to their relationship with the deceased; the cause of or circumstances surrounding the death or trauma experience; or their underestimated or misunderstood loss, grief, and trauma responses, participation in the AGL group provides an antidote to the possible isolation, loneliness, shame, guilt, anger, and confusion they may experience. "The group setting allows them to hear and identify with others' stories. Their losses deemed less significant or appropriate in general society, can be appreciated in the group. Support groups offer disenfranchised grievers a degree of recognition in a world that ignores or repudiates their grief, thus enfranchising them" (Pesek, 2002, p. 133).

CHAPTER 10

Therapeutic Activities for Working
WIth Adolescents

This chapter explores various activities that contribute therapeutic value to adolescents who are grieving death or non-death losses as well as grief and trauma experiences. The use of ritual; art work; music; construction of a loss, grief, and trauma narrative; journaling; and other specific grief-focused activities are discussed, detailing the ways in which these aid adolescents in finding or making meaning of their loss, grief, or trauma. Since adolescent loss, grief, and trauma responses are distinctly different from the loss, grief, and trauma responses of children and adults, treatment of adolescents confronting loss, grief, and trauma necessitates approaches specific to the unique needs, interests, and developmental issues of adolescence.

THE USE OF RITUAL
Rituals can be very powerful and rich in meaning. Funerals, loss anniversaries, and remembrance or memorial ceremonies and services are common examples of rituals. Rituals provide guidance about behavior, time, and emotions in response to loss (both death and non-death loss), grief, and trauma. They aid in organizing emotional expression, and they pattern behavior during a chaotic period of transition (DeVries, 1996). Rituals allow for both collective and individual expression, whether it is in the family, the school, the community, or the nation. The significance is both social and personal (Doka, 2002; 2008). Loss, grief, and trauma therapy with adolescents can focus on creating an appropriate and meaningful ritual to commemorate the death of a loved one; a trauma experience; or even a loss event such as a divorce, relocation, or school change. Therapists can offer ritual as a form of intervention and can help an adolescent

create an individualized therapeutic ritual that emerges from the narrative of the adolescent's experience of loss, grief, or trauma. It is imperative that adolescents be included in planning the ritual, because it empowers them to be part of the healing process. Rituals can be viewed as another way for adolescents to maintain continuing bonds with their deceased loved one.

The Funeral Ritual

Funeral rituals range from large gatherings of mourners to very small services that admit only family members. Funeral rituals can offer the following benefits to adolescents (Doka, 2002; Rando, 1993):

- Confirms for the adolescent the reality of the individual's death
- Allows for the adolescent's expression of grief within a contained, structured event
- Allows for recollection of the deceased, both for the individual adolescent and for groups of adolescents
- Offers an opportunity for adolescents to be actively involved in a structured activity during an emotionally disorganized time
- Provides social support to adolescent grievers within a community context
- Offers adolescents meaning for the loss, to understand death within their belief systems
- Reminds adolescents of both the reality of death and the community's ability to continue to function
- Illustrates for adolescents that this is a rite of passage as they say goodbye to the deceased's corporal form

The funeral ritual can benefit adolescents when it allows them to personalize and participate in this ritual.

Case Example

Jeremy excelled at running track in high school. He was the youngest of three children, and both his older brother and older sister ran track at college; it was expected that he would do the same. During the middle of his sophomore year in high school, Jeremy was diagnosed with an advanced form of osteosarcoma in one of his legs. He was no longer able to run, and needed crutches to navigate the school hallways. The disease progressed, and after multiple but unsuccessful treatments, Jeremy died before the end of his senior year. His family opted to invite the entire high school to his funeral service at their church, and allowed for his friends, track team, and entire student body to participate in its planning and provision. Jeremy's casket was escorted down the church aisle by his brother, sister, and track team members. After his family spoke about Jeremy, eight members of his track team gave speeches about this young man. There were two memory boards full of pictures of Jeremy. One board's photos were compiled by his family members and contained pictures of him from infancy to the present time. The other board was created by friends, track team members, and other students, and it held pictures and memorabilia from his school days. All of the school's teams came dressed in their jerseys, and band members in their uniforms. After the funeral service, students gathered together in small huddled groups as they shared stories about Jeremy. His parents went from group to group thanking the students for being a part of his life and for participating in saying goodbye to him. There were tears, hugs, and laughter evident throughout the groups of students and adults. This funeral ritual was a very community-oriented and inclusive event that allowed adolescents to both participate in and provide for it, thus enfranchising an entire school of adolescents.

Doka (2002) outlines various therapeutic rituals beyond the funeral ritual, to include rituals of continuity, rituals of transition, rituals of reconciliation, and rituals of affirmation.

Rituals of Continuity

Rituals of continuity identify the importance of the ongoing presence or impact of the loss, death, or trauma experience. Examples of this include lighting a candle on the anniversary, holiday, or birthday to commemorate a person or the loss or trauma event. This offers the adolescent an opportunity to grieve or continue to grieve, since the feelings, thoughts, and behaviors related to loss, grief, and trauma know no time limit. It gives the adolescent permission to remember and to grieve. It also provides a space for the therapist to bear witness to the adolescent's remembrance and the grief.

Case Example

At age 13, Laurie's mother died of breast cancer. Laurie, now 16 years old, celebrates her mother's birthday each year by singing happy birthday to her and buying herself a rose. "I sing and I cry. The strange thing is,

I am getting older on my birthdays but I still see her as the same on her birthday." She describes how the rose is beautiful when fresh but still beautiful in a different way when it dries out. "It kinda fades like Mom did. But she was still beautiful to me, and always will be."

Rituals of Transition
Rituals of transition indicate movement or growth in an adolescent's life. Examples of this include an adolescent achieving an academic or extra-curricular honor or award, the application and visitation process related to college, preparing for and attending prom, high school graduation, and then going on to college or the military or a job. This may also include an adolescent welcoming a stepparent and/or stepsiblings into the family.

Case Example
Latoya, a 15 year-old, was raised by her grandmother, who died this past year due to heart problems. Now it is just Latoya and her grandfather. Latoya is an artist, with hopes of attending college to further pursue art. One of her art teachers recommended her for a community project to reinvigorate the neighborhood by creating artworks in public spaces. Latoya was accepted as one of five students from local high schools. She was a member of an art team that created and painted a large mural depicting people of all ages, races, shapes, and sizes. Both grandparents were supportive of her artwork, especially her grandmother, who ensured she had the necessary materials. As a tribute to her grandmother and to include her as she transitioned from high school artist to community artist, Latoya opted to paint an older woman on the mural that closely resembled her grandmother.

Rituals of Reconciliation
Rituals of reconciliation allow people to offer or accept forgiveness, and to complete any unfinished business regarding the loss, death, or trauma experience. Examples include an adolescent writing a letter to a deceased loved one, expressing her feelings about the time period surrounding the death. This allows the therapist to bear witness to the reconciliation and to guide the adolescent toward offering or accepting forgiveness for her role or perceived role in any event that involved the deceased loved one.

Case Example
Katie is a 14 year-old struggling with a myriad of feelings she has toward her uncle, who recently died from complications related to heart

surgery. He had previously lived in a different state and visited the family whenever he was nearby touring with his band, but he sometimes went years without visiting. This uncle sexually molested Katie from ages six to ten. Katie had difficulty in 8th and 9th grades, when her academics began to suffer and she became promiscuous. This was shortly after her uncle decided to move nearby due to his health problems. Her mother forced her to attend his funeral, stating he was her only maternal uncle. Katie became angry and withdrawn, refusing to talk to her mother, who then took her to therapy. Katie eventually told all of this to her therapist, and together they explored Katie's anger, frustration, and sadness. She was angry at her mother for not protecting her, and upset with herself for not feeling sad about her uncle's death. Over time Katie began to let go of some of the anger she had at her mother and at her uncle. Together, Katie and her therapist came up with a plan for Katie to write a letter to her uncle. She did so, beginning many of her sentences with "How dare you . . ." Through this exercise she was able to access the depth of her anger. She read the letter aloud in therapy, sobbing as she did so. Afterward, she tore the letter into small pieces and threw it in the garbage. Within a few weeks, Katie brought another letter to therapy and read it aloud. In this letter, she expressed forgiveness toward her uncle, explaining that getting the anger out helped her to not give him power over her. She tore this letter into small pieces as well. After rebuilding her self-worth and doing some therapy with her mother, Katie's grades improved and she became involved in extracurricular activities at school.

Rituals of Affirmation
Rituals of affirmation offer the adolescent an opportunity to acknowledge the lessons learned and growth gained from the experience of loss, death, or trauma. These can be transformative as adolescents strive to make meaning of the loss, grief, or trauma event.

Case Example
Taylor, a 17 year-old who lived with his father until he died suddenly of an aneurysm, had to move back in with his mother and stepfather. His father drank and smoked and allowed Taylor to do the same. He was angry about having to move, hoping to find a way to afford the apartment they had lived in. However, with a low-paying job at a convenience store and still in high school, this was not possible. As he moved through his grief, Taylor began to make choices that were different than

his father's. "I loved him, he was a good man, just not a very happy or successful one. I think I need to learn something from this." He decided to improve his grades and attend community college.

LOSS, GRIEF, AND TRAUMA NARRATIVE CONSTRUCTION

Adolescents can be "assisted in constructing a coherent, temporally organized trauma narrative that includes objective and subjective features of the traumatic experience, and the worst moments of extreme fear, horror, and helplessness" (Saltzman et al., 2001, p. 52). With the therapist's guidance, the adolescent explores his thoughts about what occurred during the trauma event, to include his thinking about what he or someone else could have done to stop or intervene to prevent the injurious or lethal consequences (Saltzman et al., 2001). The worst moments of the trauma event get explored, with links made between those moments and trauma reminders. This initial narrative allows the therapist insight into the range of possible trauma reminders and trauma avoidance, which can then be used in creating a coping plan.

The adolescent is asked to talk about the trauma event, and to describe and define in exquisite detail both the objective and subjective features of the trauma event. These would include what he remembers seeing, hearing, touching, and smelling, since during a trauma event all senses can be hyperaroused. Questions are asked about these in order to obtain the specific details of each. He is also asked about his impressions, thoughts, feelings, and reactions to each of these detailed features of the trauma event. The adolescent is asked to describe the worst moments of the trauma event, and to identify what occurs in his life that reminds him of the trauma event. This enables the therapist to link those moments with trauma reminders in order to assist the adolescent in generating ideas to devise a coping plan replete with useful strategies. He is to explore his thoughts about the trauma event, to include what he or someone else could have done to stop, intervene, or prevent the consequences of the trauma event. This initial trauma narrative allows the therapist insight into the thoughts, feelings, and belief system of the adolescent. It also illustrates the range of possible trauma reminders that the adolescent is struggling with, as well as the scope of his trauma avoidance. The information gathered from the loss, grief, and trauma narrative construction aids the therapist and adolescent to work together to develop ideas for creating a healthy coping plan. Additionally, any unresolved loss and/or trauma can be worked on through integrating the processes of memory and narrative.

The therapist needs to gather precise information regarding the specific objective features of the trauma or crisis event, to include (Pynoos, Steinberg, & Goenjian, 1996):

1. To what extent was the adolescent exposed to a direct threat to his life?
2. Did the adolescent sustain any injury to herself? What was the extent of the physical pain she endured?
3. Did the adolescent witness any mutilating injury or grotesque death of anyone, especially of family members or friends?
4. Was the adolescent forced or coerced to perpetrate any violent acts against others, especially to family members or friends?
5. Did the adolescent hear unanswered screams for help and cries of distress by anyone?
6. Did the adolescent experience smelling noxious odors of any kind?
7. Was the adolescent trapped or without assistance for any period of time?
8. What was the adolescent's proximity to violent threat and violence?
9. What was the unexpectedness and duration of the trauma event for the adolescent?
10. What was the extent of violent force experienced by the adolescent, and was there use of a weapon or injurious object?
11. What were the number and nature of threats during each violent episode experienced by the adolescent?
12. Did the adolescent witness atrocities, to include torture, rape, and murder?
13. Did the adolescent witness dead bodies, especially those of family members or friends?
14. What was the adolescent's relationship to the assailant and other victims?
15. Did the adolescent experience use of physical coercion?
16. Was there violation of the physical integrity of the adolescent?
17. What was the degree of brutality or malevolence experienced by the adolescent?

All of these factors contribute to the onset and persistence of traumatic grief and loss in adolescents (Pynoos et al., 1996).

Case Example

Tyler, age 16, relocated to another city after he and his family survived Hurricane Katrina. A few months after the family's relocation, Tyler began to have nightmares, and he was subsequently brought to therapy. Over time, he slowly began to narrate his experience as a survivor of the hurricane. He described the rising water and how quickly it engulfed everything and everyone around him, stranding people on rooftops and in trees. His father was out of town for work when the storm began, leaving him with his mother and two younger sisters. They managed to pack up a few things and waded through the water. His sisters were crying because they were unable to bring their two kittens, but they convinced him to put their goldfish in a cooler to save it. The water continued to rise and run fast. Tyler, his sisters, and their mother were able to climb into the lower branches of a tree and cling to it. As they did this, he noticed the water coming faster and faster. He saw a rowboat on the other side and a few houses up of what was once a street. He describes knowing in that moment what he had to do, that he must get that boat and save his family. He did just that, but he never told his family how he actually got the boat. In therapy he talked about "bodies in the water floating by, bumping into my legs." He eventually explained how he had to fight to get the boat. He hit a man with the oar, who fell over into the water. "I don't know if he was one of the bodies floating by. I don't know if I killed him." Processing through Tyler's trauma narrative brought to light his fear of being a murderer, of the man's family tracking him down, of going to jail, and of "burning in hell." He felt tremendous guilt about the necessary actions he took to save his family. He also experienced survivor guilt due to not being able to help the people he had to pass by in the boat. He described hearing people screaming and crying out in fear. "I hear them in my dreams." Tyler becomes very anxious whenever it rains, fearful of another hurricane or flood. Over time, Tyler and his therapist were able to work through the details of his trauma narrative, integrating it with detailed memory. He learned to identify the range of trauma reminders and triggers, and to examine his thoughts and feelings about the events of that traumatic experience. Together Tyler and his therapist designed a coping plan that included relaxation and self-soothing techniques. He began to use these to self-regulate whenever he became triggered by trauma reminders.

THERAPEUTIC QUESTIONS ABOUT LOSS, GRIEF, AND TRAUMA

These therapeutic questions are designed to get at the story of an adolescent's loss, grief, or trauma experience through five specific sections.

The therapist's intention is to gather information and assess the adolescent's progression through this process. The adolescent's verbal and nonverbal answers and reactions to these questions provide insight into the adolescent's physical, social, emotional, and cognitive loss, grief, and trauma responses. In each section below, the idea is to elicit a narrative account. These therapeutic questions help the therapist to remain focused on eliciting information from the adolescent. The therapist does not ask these questions in the form of a survey, but uses them as a guide in an open-ended manner to encourage adolescents to talk freely and to share personal information in their own manner.

Section 1: Story of the Loss, Grief, or Trauma Event
- Tell me about the day of your loss, grief, and trauma experience
- Describe what happened
- Describe where you were
- Describe what you were doing
- Tell me about who was with you
- Describe your first thoughts
- Tell me about your reaction
- Tell me about your concerns at the time
- Describe what you did after your loss, grief, and trauma experience
- Tell me about seeking help/support from people

Section 2: Physical Loss, Grief, and Trauma Responses
- Describe how your body felt at the time
- Describe what and where in your body you felt it
- Tell me about your appetite following your loss, grief, and trauma experience
- Describe your sleep following your loss, grief, and trauma experience
- Tell me about how your body feels now
- Tell me about any concerns you have about your body

Section 3: Social Loss, Grief, and Trauma Responses
- Tell me about who you can talk to
- Tell me about your friends' reactions
- Tell me about family members' reactions
- Talk about who you hang out with

- Describe your alone time
- Tell me about your activities and interests

Section 4: Emotional Loss, Grief, and Trauma Responses
- Talk about how things are now for you
- Tell me about your feelings now
- Describe any worries or concerns you have

Section 5: Cognitive Loss, Grief, and Trauma Responses
- Tell me what you think about your loss, grief, and trauma experience
- Describe some things you think about
- Tell me about your concentration at school and at home after your loss, grief, and trauma experience
- Tell me about your concentration now

ART WORK

Integrating art therapy into other interventions and grief therapy milieus, to include individual, group, and family therapy, helps adolescents to communicate, understand, and cope with loss, grief, and trauma and its effects on them (Goodman, 2002). Art therapy includes drawing, painting, modeling with clay or Play-Doh, collaging, as well as creating memory boxes. Obtaining direct access to an adolescent's world can be achieved via her imagination, where thoughts, ideas, and emotions make connections with factual information (Goodman, 2002). Art therapy in conjunction with traditional talk therapy can prove extremely valuable. Therapeutic communication may be easier and at times more direct "through the use of symbols or images rather than through the complex world of spoken language" (Goodman, 2002, p. 299). "Symbols restore a sense of unity by integrating and connecting emotions, perceptions, and thoughts not previously brought into juxtaposition and, in so doing, create a complex subjective experience that is deeply moving and cathartic" (Lewis & Langer, 1994, p. 232). The integration of art therapy can also strengthen the therapeutic relationship by allowing an adolescent to speak her own language in her own time and in her own fashion.

Case Example

Jason's 16 year-old twin sister died in a scuba diving accident when the family was on vacation over the previous summer. Described as typically an outgoing, fun-loving extrovert, his parents were concerned about his isolation and tendency to withdraw. They understood that he was grieving his sister, his very best friend, and that they too were grieving, but said that he seemed "stuck in solitude." Jason was quiet and withdrawn in his first few therapy sessions, not having much to say other than yes of course he was very, very sad and that he missed his sister "more than words can say." His therapist suggested creating a collage of his thoughts and feelings about his sister. Jason agreed to give it a try. He was given a poster board and a pile of magazines. He spent the next two sessions cutting out magazine pictures and words and putting them into piles. He drew a line across the middle of the poster board and began to collage. Jason's completed collage showed the sky above, "the air I breathe," and the sea below, "the water she inhaled." He pasted pictures and words in each half, creating a beautiful, magical seascape consisting of animals "because she had a real soft spot for all kinds of animals," and colored in blues and greens, "her favorite colors," with gel pens. He also pasted in pictures of flowers "because they are so her." Some of the words Jason chose to paste in the sea were "freedom," "heaven," "art," "floral," "play," "hands down," and "a world of good." Some of these were whole words and others made up from individual letters. He drew and pasted storm clouds and lightning in the sky and added words such as "anger," "fault," "remote," "alone," and "just me." Jason talked as he did this, describing the last moments of his sister's life when he knew she would not make it. "Something happened, and she was just sort of floating there. I knew she was dead, and I couldn't stop looking at her. I see her in my dreams just floating like that."

Collage can be "a viable healing modality" that can "unlock doors to unexplored feelings" (Strouse, 2014, p. 196). This creative endeavor allows for the emergence of multiple meanings in response to an adolescent's thoughts and feelings related to loss, grief, and trauma.

BIBLIOTHERAPY

The use of literature can be a very powerful intervention and life-enhancing therapeutic approach with adolescents who like to read. Much of the current young adult (YA) fiction focuses on the challenges and choices faced by many adolescents, both male and female. Many of them involve themes of loss, grief, and trauma and how adolescents work through their thoughts and feelings. There are certainly limitations to the utilization of bibliotherapy with adolescents. It should be used as an adjunct to the therapeutic work provided by a therapist rather than a main focus of treatment. However, it can provide a focal point for discussion and a pathway to an adolescent's internal world.

MUSIC AS CONNECTION

Adolescents utilize music as both a method of emotional expression and as a way to connect to their own emotions. It can both mirror and alter their feelings of anger, sadness, hope, betrayal, loneliness, and confusion, to name a few. As previously mentioned, adolescents can be reluctant to show strong emotions and may appear as doing better than they really are. Listening to and making music can act as a conduit between their personal or internal self and their public or external self. Music can play an important role in representing the true but often hidden feelings of adolescents confronted with loss, grief, and trauma (McFerran, Roberts, & O'Grady, 2010). Activities that involve music can be done individually with an adolescent and/or with a group of adolescents. Music can offer a nonthreatening, even safe or at least familiar, environment in which to work on loss, grief, and trauma. Since music affects emotional and physical well-being, adolescents tend to use it to alter or manage their moods. Listening to sad songs can evoke tears as a cathartic method to express grief. Listening to upbeat music can create a respite from sadness and anger. Listening to loud and fast music can help access anger and other strong emotions. Adolescents can create categorical playlists such as soothing/relaxing music, sad music, uplifting/joyful music, angry music, or reminiscent music. Playlists can be created and stored on an adolescent's cell phone, tablet, or laptop to be easily accessed throughout his day.

Music is used not just for expressive or emotionally related purposes, but for meaning making as well. Listening to meaningful music is very important for adolescents. Often it is the lyric content that captures an adolescent's interest. Therapists can listen to and analyze the meaning of the lyrics with an adolescent, which can provide "an effective structure for grief counseling" (Wlodarczyk, 2014). One adolescent girl described her need to hear lyrics that spoke to her; she no longer listened to pop songs because they were too superficial. As described by 15 year-old Tanisha, who prefers to spend time alone in her room after a classmate died in a fatal motorcycle accident, "To listen to music, but it's not like superficial music that you hear on the radio stations. It's more deep, more real, more about life and stuff." This asserts that music has great significance throughout adolescence (Shaller & Smith, 2002).

Research on adolescents who participated in a music therapy group resulted in the adolescents reporting five areas in which they were given permission to grieve (McFerran et al., 2010). These adolescents experienced changes in their grieving status in which they engaged with their feelings and thoughts of loss and grief as a way to move through it rather than holding on to it. Another area of change was in their loss-related feelings, which were released through both writing and playing music. The music therapy group provided an environment in which to both release and get relief from their daily experience of loss and grief, which in turn enabled them to cope outside of school. The adolescents reported an improved connection between themselves and others in that they felt heard, held, and understood by other group members, which decreased their sense of loneliness and isolation. Finally, there was an increase in their levels of sharing about their loss outside of the group, which initially emerged as taking an emotional risk to disclose about their loss and grief within the music group (McFerran et al., 2010). Another study demonstrates that bereaved adolescents involved in a songwriting-based clinical music therapy protocol experienced positive growth, with improvement in all grief-processing domains to include areas of understanding, feelings, remembering, integrating, and growing (Dalton & Krout, 2005).

Berger (2012, pp. 211–212) outlines a "repertoire of playlist questions" to begin with narrative storytelling that include:

What were _____ (your loved one's) favorite pieces of music?
When did you experience these together?
What do you miss about those times?
If you were to create a movie about your loss, what music would you use on its soundtrack?
What music best describes your experience of loss?

This outline of questions can prove very useful in therapy with adolescents, who typically enjoy compiling playlists.

Case Example

Caleb, age 15, began therapy about four months after his mother died of breast cancer. Hers was an anticipated death that involved an illness that spanned about two years. Caleb is an only child, and now it is just he and his father, with no extended family in the state where they reside. He describes having many friends at school through his extracurricular activities on the debate team and playing on the soccer team. Yet he also describes an overpowering loneliness and a sense of being different and apart from his friends. They all have mothers and he does not. When asked what he does to manage the loneliness, he mentions that he listens to music. On further exploration, he discusses the playlist he compiled for his mother as she was dying, and that he listens to it when he feels especially lonely and misses her. He asks for permission to play some of it in the therapy session, and does so. He listens to a beautiful combination of classical music, folk, and country. Caleb states that he changes the playlist from time to time to include music that simply reminds him of his mother rather than her favorite songs. It turns out he listens to songs with very empowering and meaningful lyrics that allow him to access his emotions. Sometimes he just wants a cathartic cry while other times he wants to feel bolstered by the lyrics. After compiling a few different playlists, Caleb decides to create one for his father about his mother.

JOURNALING

Journaling can be an effective method for recognizing, acknowledging, naming, expressing, and moving through the panoply of emotions related to loss, grief, and trauma. Use of open-ended sentences, prompts, statements, and quotes can aid adolescents in accessing their thoughts and feelings in response to loss, grief, and trauma. The following are some sentence starters to be used individually or in an adolescent group:

If only . . .	I want . . .	I don't want . . .
I wish . . .	I feel sad when . . .	I feel angry when . . .
If I could . . .	I feel lonely when . . .	I feel ashamed when . . .
How dare . . .	I like . . .	I hate . . .
I will . . .	I am . . .	It helps to . . .
It hurts to . . .		

LOSS HISTORY TIMELINE

Each person develops her own unique style of coping with loss, grief, and trauma. Adolescents are at the very beginning of the process of forming attitudes, values, and reactions to their experience of loss, grief, or trauma. They may very well carry these into adulthood, with some adolescents having developed better and healthier coping skills than others. This activity asks an adolescent to think about all kinds of loss, grief, and trauma she has experienced thus far in life, and it can be completed in between sessions or during a session. On an 8″ × 11″ piece of paper turned horizontally, the adolescent is asked to construct a Loss History Timeline as follows:

Age at time of loss
_____
Type of loss or trauma, dates and any other significant information

The benefit of the Loss History Timeline is that it gives a pictorial representation of an adolescent's loss, grief, and trauma experiences, connecting points in time. It acts as an assessment tool for the therapist to use to discuss with an adolescent how she has coped with each loss, grief, and trauma experience. Together they can determine if there are any remaining grief or trauma issues or unfinished business related to each. They can also learn more about the adolescent's personal style of dealing with loss, grief, and trauma by examining what influences her coping style, such as the people in her life and her cultural, ethnic, and religious background. Additionally, the therapist can take a close look at the adolescent's coping strategies, strengths, and resources, both internal and external, to determine what has and has not benefited her in the past.

Case Example

Marissa began individual therapy at age 12 to learn to manage her emotional and behavioral responses to multiple loss, grief, and trauma experiences. When she began therapy, she used nonlethal self-injury in the form of cutting on her arms as a coping method for emotional regulation of intense feelings. The Loss History Timeline was a therapeutic exercise employed only after Marissa was no longer cutting and had integrated healthy self-soothing and grounding techniques into her daily routine. After much loss and grief work had been accomplished, her therapist determined Marissa was ready to complete this exercise. Below is an example of Marissa's Loss History Timeline at age 17:

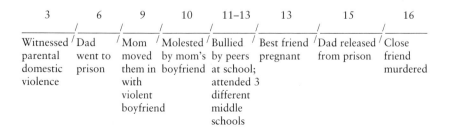

3	6	9	10	11–13	13	15	16
Witnessed parental domestic violence	Dad went to prison	Mom moved them in with violent boyfriend	Molested by mom's boyfriend	Bullied by peers at school; attended 3 different middle schools	Best friend pregnant	Dad released from prison	Close friend murdered

In this pictorial representation of Marissa's loss, grief, and trauma experiences, both death and non-death losses are noted. She first created her Loss History Timeline at age 12, and then again at age 17. Her first trauma experience, at age three, was witnessing the domestic violence between her parents, which created a non-death loss regarding a sense of safety and security. She was not able to fully articulate this when she began therapy at age 12, but she did allude to not trusting her father. Her mother described a horrific scene where Marissa saw her father beat her mother. Her parents were in the front seat of the car parked in the driveway, Marissa was in the back seat, and as stated by her mother, "Saw blood go everywhere as he punched my face into a bloody nothing and broke my jaw." At age six, Marissa's father was incarcerated for assault. Between ages six and 13, she was forced by her grandparents to visit him at prison. She describes how her mother moved them in and out of her grandparents' home. At age nine her mother's boyfriend, with whom they were living, became violent toward her mother and threatening toward Marissa, creating another unsafe and insecure living arrangement. At age 10, her mother's same violent boyfriend sexually molested her, which added to her loss of feeling safe and secure not only in the home but in her body as well. Throughout her middle school years, ages 11 to 13, Marissa was bullied by female classmates, which made it difficult for her to feel safe at school, which affected her attendance. It was at this time that she began nonlethal self-injury by cutting on her arms. By the time she entered high school, she had attended three different middle schools as a way of escaping from the bullying. However, she lost the few friends she had, and decided that making new friends was not a safe endeavor. During the summer between middle school and high school, her best friend had a baby, which changed their friendship since there was no longer time to just hang out and have sleepovers. This resulted in more non-death friendship loss. By her sophomore year in high school, Marissa had stopped cutting, tried out for and made the cheerleading squad, and made some friends through her cheering. When she was age 15, her father was released from prison and wanted to spend time with her. In doing so, Marissa experienced more non-death loss regarding this relationship in realizing he did not know her, he did not want to engage in activities to get to know her, and that he would never be the father she had hoped for. At age 16, Marissa was part of a friendship group with some of the cheerleaders, and she reconnected with her friend who was now the mother of a three year-old son. During her junior year of high school, that friend was murdered, creating a tragic and painful loss for Marissa and her friends.

When Marissa first created her Loss History Timeline at age 12, she and her therapist used it as an assessment tool to look at the ways in which she coped with loss, grief, and trauma. Marissa tended to withdraw, isolate, and inflict nonlethal self-injury in the form of cutting. She did this when she was hurt but mostly when she was angry and was overwhelmed by the intensity of her anger. In examining how she developed her personal style of dealing with loss, grief, and trauma, it became evident that she learned from her mother's very stoic family to not talk about problems or troubles and not to show her emotions. "You don't have to go very far to find someone having it worse than you" was her family motto. Her father's emotional style was the opposite of her mother's; he exploded and became violent when angry. Neither of these were beneficial coping strategies for Marissa, who learned to turn her feelings inward and self-injure, mostly when angry. In therapy Marissa found an acceptable and emotionally safe environment in which to talk about and explore her thoughts, feelings, and behavior related to loss, grief, and trauma. She exhibited excellent verbal skills and insight, which became her strengths. In doing the Loss History Timeline at two different age points, and discussing it at length with her therapist, Marissa found this to be an extremely useful activity in examining her internal and external strengths and resources.

BODY MAP

The creation of a Body Map is a particularly powerful activity for an adolescent who has experienced physical trauma of any kind related to an accident, assault, sexual or physical abuse, or medical/surgical procedure. This activity is a way for an adolescent to attune to and explore loss, grief, and trauma feelings related to her physical self. This powerful activity allows for both the depiction and description of embodied pain. It introduces an enactment of loss, grief, and trauma through expressive art. This can be done in an individual, group, or family therapy setting. The first step involves asking the adolescent to lie down on a large piece of paper and, with her permission, outlining her body. The therapist provides colored pens, crayons, markers, glitter, Band-Aids, and materials that include both softness such as feathers, felt, and thread, and hardness such as stones, staples, and pushpins. The adolescent then begins to decorate her Body Map with words, color, and the available soft and hard materials. As the adolescent maps the body, she can do so quietly, listen to music, or narrate the process. After the Body Map is completed, the adolescent is asked to describe the finished image.

Case Example

Chelsea was brought to therapy at age 17 to help her manage the anger and sadness she felt in response to the surgical loss of her left leg to just above her knee. She was diagnosed with osteosarcoma, a cancer of the bone, which necessitated surgery the previous year. She had finished chemotherapy, was on crutches, and a plan was in place to begin physical therapy and fitting for a prosthetic leg. Complicating this loss was the fact that Chelsea had been a dancer since the age of six. Over the years, she was a regular in many ballet and modern dance performances with the local junior ballet company, danced the role of Clara in the Nutcracker in the senior ballet company, and planned a career as a professional dancer. Prior to diagnosis, she was scheduled to study with a national ballet company over the summer, hoping this would launch her professional dance career.

The Body Map activity was explained to Chelsea, who agreed to give it a try. She continued to have great agility even with one leg, and was able to lower herself to the piece of paper for the outlining of her body. When she sat up and looked at the outline, she stated, "As you can see, I only have half a leg there. That's what makes me meanly mad. I'll never dance again." She began decorating her Body Map with vigor. She described her Body Map as a representation of how she felt, "Half dead and half alive." She began by drawing a black line down the middle of her Body Map. Chelsea's right half of her Body Map was a ballerina. She colored that half in a pink leotard and frilly tutu, along with her foot in a pink toe shoe. She made up her right eye to be large and blue, with gold glitter eye shadow, dark eyeliner, and long dark eyelashes. There was a spot of rouge on her right cheek, and half of her smiling mouth had pink lipstick. She drew a pink heart encircled with silver glitter in her right hand. The right half of her hair was colored shimmery yellow, piled up on top of her head, with half of a glittery silver tiara. Chelsea's left half of her Body Map had a big black stone for an eye, long bits of yellow thread for hair, and a black straight line for her mouth. She drew and colored in a baggy gray sweatshirt over the left side of her body, and in her left hand drew a red heart encircled with what she described as black thorns. She drew a black toe shoe at the bottom of where her left foot would have been, and glued small black stones on top of it. She then used a black marker and forcefully drew a large ragged line between her knee area and the black toe shoe. She tore through the paper as she did this. "I don't know what to do with either part of my body. I feel alive when I think about dancing yet dead at the same time. This is me now. Half dead and half alive. I should feel good about even being alive. I know my future is uncertain with this cancer. I'm just so angry at that leg, that leg that's gone. I miss dancing and that makes me feel so selfish when I could die and not even be with my family."

Chelsea and her therapist discussed her Body Map with a focus on the emotional content as she described her dyadic half dead/half alive thought process. It became clear that she felt torn between trying to enjoy the life she still had and the fear and uncertainty regarding her prognosis. "I should be content to be here 'cause I could still die, but I'm not."

EMPTY CHAIR

This Gestalt therapy technique has been used in therapeutic settings since Perls first introduced the concept. After therapeutic rapport has been established over the period of time necessary, the therapist can bring up and describe the idea of doing an empty chair exercise. This can be an especially powerful and vivid "experiential intervention that invites immediacy and vulnerability with the deceased" (Neimeyer, 2012, p. 272).

Case Example

Miranda, age 18, came to therapy in response to her 20 year-old sister Morgan's death by suicide three weeks prior. This not only overshadowed her upcoming high school graduation but also postponed a family trip to Europe planned during the previous couple of years. In describing the recent events, anger radiated from her entire being. "I am just so angry at her. How selfish! I cannot believe she did this. I feel sorry for my parents, especially my dad, they were so close, but I am furious. Is that wrong of me? She was just such a mess. Always was. Always causing problems. Always a problem." Miranda and her therapist worked for some weeks before her therapist brought up the idea of doing an empty chair exercise. Miranda willingly agreed to try it. She was instructed to imagine her sister in one of the chairs either across from her or to her left. She opted to put her sister in the chair across from her. "I am so angry at you. Why did you do this? And why now? We planned a vacation together. The whole family." Miranda was then instructed to sit in the opposite chair and respond as Morgan. "Well, I'm sorry. I'm so sorry for so much. I really tried. I tried to live. I just couldn't do it any more. I know you'll never understand. No one understood how I felt. Just so bad all the time." At this point Miranda asked if she could stop. After she moved back into her own chair, she said that Morgan was right, that she could never understand how bad she always felt. "I am just so sorry there was nothing I could do for her. No one could. I hope she's at peace. I guess she just couldn't hang on for Europe. I'm gonna go there some day and enjoy it for her."

It takes courage for an adolescent to agree to the empty chair exercise. It can be a powerful dramatization of the internalized relationship between the adolescent and their deceased loved one. Empty "chair work can promote healing conversations with the self and deceased that transcend even the silence of the grave" (Neimeyer, 2012, p. 272).

MEMORY BOX

A memory box is a container that holds symbols or creative representations of a particular loss, as well as the idea of the loss of an assumptive, previously known, and safe world. Memory boxes are used to store prized mementos that remind an adolescent of his deceased loved one. Since memory boxes provide a contained space, an adolescent "can choose when to open and explore their contents, thereby providing a perceived sense of control. They are also organic spaces, as contents can be added, removed, or replaced" (Potash & Handel, 2012, p. 243). This therapeutic activity can be done in a group or an individual therapy setting. The therapist provides the materials for decorating the memory box and may also provide the container. Materials would include magazines for cutting out pictures; glue sticks; gel pens; and small objects such as marbles, buttons, lace, colored string, glitter, and decorative confetti in various shapes and forms. Materials for containers could include a shoe box, cigar box, or various sized packing boxes. The adolescent is instructed to bring some items from home that remind him of his deceased loved one. The adolescent is encouraged to be creative in using the various materials and objects to design a container that communicates and represents his loss. After he completes construction and decoration of his memory box, the adolescent is then given the opportunity to explain the meaning that it holds for him as well as describe what he thought and felt during the process.

Case Example

When 13 year-old Sam's grandfather died from lung cancer, Sam had difficulty talking to his parents about his feelings. He was extremely close to his grandfather, having created a strong bond during the time Sam's father was deployed to Afghanistan. Sam became withdrawn and quiet, preferring to walk around their rural property and spend time at their stock pond where he and his grandfather fished. The memory box activity was explained to Sam after he saw his therapist a few times. He was instructed to bring in some items that reminded him of his grandfather, and he spent three one-hour therapy sessions constructing and decorating his memory box. Once completed, he smiled and stated, "There. That's him!" The outside of Sam's memory box (a shoe box) was decorated with twigs, stones, and moss that he had collected from walking around his home. Pictures glued to the inside portrayed a tractor, deer, some cattle, camouflaged clothing, and a hand drawing of a rattlesnake. There were some loose items that included two fishing lures, a smooth rock, a small pocketknife, and a photo of Sam and his grandfather next to a barn. "These are things I liked to do with Grandpa. I like to be outside doing stuff and he did too."

CONCLUSION

This book was intended to provide a guide for therapists and others interested in working with adolescents as they try to make sense of the loss, grief, and trauma experiences in their lives. My intention was to present a variety of approaches and techniques to utilize in working with adolescents based on the physical, social, emotional, and cognitive developmental needs of adolescents. The response of adolescents to loss, grief, and trauma experiences is intimately related to these developmental domains, and both their strengths and challenges must be looked at from this perspective. Adolescents must have the reality of their grief validated and normalized, even though they may struggle mightily to camouflage their feelings. Engaging them in a variety of therapeutic techniques and activities, and respecting the role of technology and social media in their lives, can help therapists gain access to how their worldview has been impacted by loss, grief, and trauma and to the most beneficial ways to guide them as they navigate the new normal of a terrain forever altered by these experiences.

REFERENCES

Ahrons, C.R. (2007). Family ties after divorce: Long-term implications for children. *Family Process, 46*(1), 53–65.

Amato, P.R. (2000). The consequences of divorce for adults and children. *Journal of Marriage and Family, 62*(4), 1269–1287.

Amato, P.R., & Anthony, C.J. (2014). The effects of parental divorce with fixed effects models. *Journal of Marriage and Family, 76*, 370–386.

Amato, P.R., & Hohmann-Marriott, B. (2007). A comparison of high- and low-distress marriages that end in divorce. *Journal of Marriage and Family, 69*, 621–638.

Anderson, S.F., Salk, R.H., & Hyde, J.S. (2015). Stress in romantic relationships and adolescent depressive symptoms: Influence of parental support. *Journal of Family Psychology, 29*(3), 339–348.

Armour, M. (2003). Meaning making in the aftermath of homicide. *Death Studies, 27*, 519–540.

Arnett, J.J. (2006). Emerging adulthood: Understanding the new way of coming of age. In J.J. Arnett & J.L. Tanner (Eds.), *Emerging adults in America: Coming of age in the 21st century* (pp. 3–20). Washington, DC: American Psychological Association Press.

Aronson, S.M. (2004). Where the wild things are: The power and challenge of adolescent group work. *The Mount Sinai Journal of Medicine, 71*(3), 174–180.

Balk, D.E. (1983). Adolescents' grief reactions and self-concept perceptions following grief: A study of 33 teenagers. *Journal of Youth and Adolescence, 12*(2), 137–161.

Balk, D.E. (1996). Models for understanding adolescent coping with bereavement. *Death Studies, 20*(4), 367–387.

Balk, D.E. (2008). The adolescent's encounter with death. In K.J. Doka & A.S. Tucci (Eds.), *Living with grief: Children and adolescents* (pp. 25–42). Washington, DC: Hospice Foundation of America.

Balk, D.E. (2009). Sibling bereavement during adolescence. In D.E. Balk & C.A. Corr (Eds.), *Adolescent encounters with death, bereavement, and coping* (pp. 199–216). New York: Springer Publishing.

Balk, D.E. (2014). *Dealing with dying, death, and grief during adolescence.* New York: Routledge.

Balk, D.E., & Corr, C.A. (1996). Adolescents, developmental tasks, and encounters with death and bereavement. In C.A. Corr & D.E. Balk (Eds.), *Handbook of adolescent death and bereavement* (pp. 3–24). New York: Springer Publishing.

Barrett, R.K. (1996). Adolescents, homicidal violence, and death. In C.A. Corr & D.E. Balk (Eds.), *Handbook of adolescent death and bereavement* (pp. 42–64). New York: Springer Publishing.

Bearman, P.S., & Moody, J. (2004). Suicide and friendship among American adolescents. *American Journal of Public Health, 94*(1), 89–95.

Berger, J.S. (2012). Playing with playlists. In R.A. Neimeyer (Ed.), *Techniques of grief therapy: Creative practices for counseling the bereaved* (pp. 211–214). New York: Routledge.

Bernstein, A.C. (2006). Re-visioning, restructuring, and reconciliation: Clinical practice with complex post-divorce families. *Family Process, 46*(1), 67–78.

Blaze, J.T., & Shwalb, D.W. (2009). Resource loss and relocation: A follow-up study of adolescents two years after Hurricane Katrina. *Psychological Trauma: Theory, Research, Practice, and Policy, 1*, 312–322.

Bonanno, G.A. (2001). Grief and emotion: A social-functional perspective. In M.S. Stroebe, R.O. Hansson, W. Stroebe, & H. Schut (Eds.), *Handbook of bereavement research: Consequences, coping, and care* (pp. 493–516). Washington, DC: American Psychological Association.

Booth, A., & Amato, P.R. (2001). Parental predivorce relations and offspring post-divorce well-being. *Journal of Marriage and Family, 63*(1), 197–212.

Bowlby, J. (1980). *Attachment and loss: Volume III. Loss, sadness, and depression.* New York: Basic Books.

Brown, B., Richards, H., & Wilson, C. (1996). Pet bonding and pet bereavement among adolescents. *Journal of Counseling and Development, 74*(5), 505–509.

Brown, L.M., & Gilligan, C. (1992). *Meeting at the crossroads.* New York: Ballantine Books.

Carmack, B.J., & Packman, W. (2011). Pet loss: The interface of continuing bonds research and practice. In R.A Neimeyer, D.L. Harris, H.R. Winokuer, & G.F. Thornton (Eds.), *Grief and bereavement in contemporary society: Bridging research and practice* (pp. 273–284). New York: Routledge.

Catone, W.V., & Schatz, M.T. (1991). The crisis moment: A school's response to the event of a suicide. *School Psychology International, 12*, 17–23.

Centers for Disease Control and Prevention. (2013). www.cdc.gov.

Cerel, J., & Aldrich, R.S. (2011). The impact of suicide on children and adolescents. In J.R. Jordan & J.L. McIntosh (Eds.), *Grief after suicide: Understanding the consequences and caring for the survivors* (pp. 81–92). New York: Routledge.

Chapman, M.V. (2003). Social support and loss during adolescence: How different are teen girls from boys? *Journal of Human Behavior in the Social Environment, 7*(3/4), 5–21.

Choate, L.H. (2014). *Adolescent girls in distress: A guide for mental health treatment and prevention.* New York: Springer.

Chowns, G. (2014). "Until it ends, you never know . . .": Attending to the voice of adolescents who are facing the likely death of a parent. *Bereavement Care, 32*(1), 23–30.

Christ, G. (2000). Impact of development on children's mourning. *Cancer Practice, 8*(2), 72–81.

Clarke-Stewart, K.A., Vangell, D.L., McCartney, K., Owen, M.T., & Booth, C. (2000). Effects of parental separation and divorce on very young children. *Journal of Family Psychology, 14*(2), 304–326.

Cohen, C.S. (1995). Making it happen: From great idea to successful support group. *Social Work with Groups, 18*(1), 67–80.

Cohen, G.J. (2002). Helping children and families deal with divorce and separation. *Pediatrics, 110*(5), 1019–1023.

Compas, B.E., Connor-Smith, J.K., Saltzman, H., Thomsen, A.H., & Wadsworth, M.E. (2001). Coping with stress during childhood and adolescence: Problems, progress, and potential in theory and research. *Psychological Bulletin, 127*, 87–127.

Corder, B.F., Whiteside, L., & Haizlip, T.M. (1981). A study of curative factors in group psychotherapy with adolescents. *International Journal of Group Psychotherapy, 31*(3), 345–354.

Corr, C.A., & Balk, D.E. (1996). Adolescents, developmental tasks, and encounters with death and bereavement. In C.A. Corr & D.E. Balk (Eds.), *Handbook of adolescent death and bereavement* (pp. 3–24). New York: Springer Publishing.

Crawford, J. (2003). Alternative sentencing necessary for female inmates with children. *Corrections Today, 65*(3), 8–11.

Dahl, R.E., & Spear, L.P. (2004). Adolescent brain development: A period of vulnerabilities and opportunities. *Annals of the New York Academy of Sciences, 1021*, 1–22.

Dalton, T.A., & Krout, R.E. (2005). Development of the Grief Process Scale through music therapy songwriting with bereaved adolescents. *The Arts in Psychotherapy, 32*, 131–143.

Dane, B. (2004). Integrating spirituality and religion. In J. Berzoff & P.R. Silverman (Eds.), *Living with dying: A handbook for end-of-life healthcare practitioners* (pp. 424–438). New York: Columbia University Press.

Davies, P.T., & Cummings, E.M. (1994). Marital conflict and child adjustment: An emotional security hypothesis. *Psychological Bulletin, 116*(3), 387–411.

Davila, J. (2008). Depressive symptoms and adolescent romance: Theory, research and implications. *Child Development Perspectives, 2*(1), 26–31.

Davis, C.G. (2001). The tormented and transformed: Understanding responses to loss and trauma. In R.A. Neimeyer (Ed.), *Meaning reconstruction & the experience of loss* (pp. 137–155). Washington, DC: American Psychological Association.

DeGroot, J.M. (2012). Maintaining relational continuity with the deceased on Facebook. *OMEGA, 65*(3), 195–212.

DeVries, M.W. (1996). Trauma in cultural perspective. In B.A. van der Kolk, A.C. McFarlane, & L. Weisaeth (Eds.), *Traumatic stress: The effects of overwhelming experience on mind, body, and society* (pp. 398–413). New York: The Guilford Press.

Doka, K.J. (Ed.). (2002). *Disenfranchised grief: New directions, challenges, and strategies for practice.* Champaign, IL: Research Press.

Doka, K.J. (2008). The power of ritual: A gift for children and adolescents. In K.J. Doka & A.S. Tucci (Eds.), *Living with grief: Children and adolescents* (pp. 287–295). Washington, DC: Hospice Foundation of America.

Doka, K.J., & Martin, T.L. (2010). *Grieving beyond gender: Understanding the ways men and women mourn.* New York: Routledge.

Drumm, K. (2006). The essential power of group work. *Social Work with Groups, 29*(2/3), 17–31.

Dyregrov, A., Gjestad, R., Wikander, A.M.B., & Vigerust, S. (1999). Reactions following the sudden death of a classmate. *Scandinavian Journal of Psychology, 40*(3), 167–176.

Emery, R.E., & Forehand, R. (1996). Parental divorce and children's well-being: A focus on resilience. In R.J. Haggerty, L.R. Sherrod, N. Garmezy, & M. Rutter (Eds.), *Stress, risk, and resilience in children and adolescents: Processes, mechanisms, and interventions* (pp. 64–99). New York: Cambridge University Press.

Ens, C., & Bond, J.B. (2007). Death anxiety in adolescents: The contributions of bereavement and religiosity. *OMEGA, 55*(3), 169–184.

Ewalt, P.L., & Perkins, L. (1979). The real experience of death among adolescents: An empirical study. *Social Casework, 60*(9), 547–551.

Fleming, S., & Balmer, L. (1996). Bereavement in adolescents. In C.A. Corr & D.E. Balk (Eds.), *Handbook of adolescent death and bereavement* (pp. 139–154). New York: Springer Publishing.

Fleming, S., & Robinson, P. (2001). Grief and cognitive-behavioral therapy: The reconstruction of meaning. In M.S. Stroebe, R.O. Hansson, W. Stroebe, & H. Schut (Eds.), *Handbook of bereavement research: Consequences, coping, and care* (pp. 647–670). Washington, DC: American Psychological Association.

Garland, J., Jones, H., & Kolodny, R. (1973). A model for stages of development in social work groups. In S. Bernstein (Ed.), *Exploration in group work* (pp. 17–71). Boston: Milford House.

Gerrity, D.A., & DeLucia-Waack, J.L. (2007). Effectiveness of groups in the schools. *Journal for Specialists in Group Work, 22*, 97–106.

Gilligan, C. (1982). *In a different voice: Psychological theory and women's development.* Cambridge, MA: Harvard University Press.

Gitterman, A. (2004). The mutual aid model. In C. Garvin, M. Galinsky, & L. Gutierrez (Eds.), *Handbook of social work with groups* (pp. 93–110). New York: Oxford Press.

Gitterman, A., & Shulman, L. (2005). The life model, oppression, vulnerability, resilience, mutual aid, and the mediating function. In A. Gitterman & L. Shulman (Eds.), *Mutual aid groups, vulnerable & resilient populations, and the life cycle* (pp. 3–37). New York: Columbia University Press.

Glodich, A., & Allen, J.G. (1998). Adolescents exposed to violence and abuse: A review of the group therapy literature with an emphasis on preventing trauma reenactment. *Journal of Child and Adolescent Group Therapy, 8*(4), 135–154.

Goodkin, K., Baldewicz, T.T., Blaney, N.T., Asthana, D., Kumar, M., Shapshak, P., Leeds, B., Burkhalter, J.E., Rigg, D., Tyll, M.D., Cohen, J., & Zheng, W.L. (2001). Physiological effects of bereavement and bereavement support group interventions. In M.S. Stroebe, R.O. Hansson,

W. Stroebe, & H. Schut (Eds.), *Handbook of bereavement research: Consequences, coping, and care* (pp. 671–704). Washington, DC: American Psychological Association.

Goodman, R.F. (2002). Art as a component of grief work with children. In K.J. Doka (Ed.), *Disenfranchised grief: New directions, challenges, and strategies for practice* (pp. 297–322). Champaign, IL: Research Press.

Gore, S., & Eckenrode, J. (1996). Context and process in research on risk and resilience. In R.J. Haggerty, L.R. Sherrod, N. Garmezy, & M. Rutter (Eds.), *Stress, risk, and resilience in children and adolescents* (pp. 19–63). New York: Cambridge University Press.

Gray, R.E. (1987). Adolescent response to the death of a parent. *Journal of Youth and Adolescence, 16*(6), 511–525.

Ha, T., Overbeek, G., Lichtwarck-Aschoff, A., & Engels, R.C.M. (2013). Do conflict resolution and recovery predict the survival of adolescents' romantic relationships? *Public Library of Science ONE, 8*(4), e61871.

Hansel, T.C., Osofsky, J.D., Osofsky, H.J., & Friedrich, P. (2013). The effect of long-term relocation on child and adolescent survivors of Hurricane Katrina. *Journal of Traumatic Stress, 26,* 613–620.

Hanson, M., Tiberius, R., Hodges, B., Mackay, S., McNaughton, N., Dickens, S., & Regehr, G. (2002). Implications of suicide contagion for the selection of adolescent standardized patients. *Academic Medicine, 77*(10), S100–S102.

Harris, E. (1991). Adolescent bereavement following the death of a parent: An exploratory study. *Child Psychiatry and Human Development, 21*(4), 267–281.

Hawkins, D. (1995). Controlling crime before it happens: Risk-focused prevention. *National Institute of Justice Journal, 229,* 10–18.

Hill, D.C., & Foster, Y.M. (1996). Postvention with early and middle adolescents. In C.A. Corr & D.E. Balk (Eds.), *Handbook of adolescent death and bereavement* (pp. 250–272). New York: Springer.

Hogan, N.S., & DeSantis, L. (1996). Adolescent sibling bereavement: Toward a new theory. In C.A. Corr & D.E. Balk (Eds.), *Handbook of adolescent death and bereavement* (pp. 173–195). New York: Springer.

Hooyman, N.R., & Kramer, B.J. (2006). *Living through loss: Interventions across the life span.* New York: Columbia University Press.

Hope, C., & Ryan, J. (2014). *Digital arts: An introduction to new media.* New York: Bloomsbury.

James, L., Oltjenbruns, K.A., & Whiting, P. (2008). Grieving adolescents: The paradox of using technology for support. In K.J. Doka & A.S. Tucci (Eds.), *Living with grief: Children and adolescents* (pp. 299–316). Washington, DC: Hospice Foundation of America.

Johnson, E.I., & Easterling, B.A. (2015). Coping with confinement: Adolescents' experiences with parental incarceration. *Journal of Adolescent Research, 30*(2), 244–267.

Jones, S. (2004). 404 not found: The Internet and the afterlife. *OMEG, 49*(1), 83–88.

Jordan, J.R., & McIntosh, J.L. (2011). Is suicide bereavement different? Perspectives from research and practice. In R.A Neimeyer, D.L. Harris, H.R. Winokuer, & G.F. Thornton (Eds.), *Grief and bereavement in contemporary society: Bridging research and practice* (pp. 223–234). New York: Routledge.

Jordan, J.V. (2003). Relational-cultural therapy. In K. Kopala & M.A. Keitel (Eds.), *Handbook of counseling women* (pp. 22–30). Thousand Oaks, CA: Sage.

Kaczmarek, M.G., & Backlund, B.A. (1991). Disenfranchised grief: The loss of an adolescent romantic relationship. *Adolescence, 26*(102), 253–260.

Kandt, V.E. (1994). Adolescent bereavement: Turning a fragile time into acceptance and peace. *School Counselor, 41*(3), 203–212.

Kasket, E. (2012). Continuing bonds in the age of social networking: Facebook as a modern-day medium. *Bereavement Care, 31*(2), 62–69.

Keeley, M., & Generous, M.A. (2014). Advice from children and adolescents on final conversations with dying loved ones. *Death Studies, 38*(5), 308–314.

Kelly, J.B. (2007). Children's living arrangements following separation and divorce: Insights from empirical and clinical research. *Family Process, 46,* 35–52.

Klass, D., Silverman, P.R., & Nickman, S.L. (Eds.). (1996). *Continuing bonds: New understandings of grief.* Washington, DC: Taylor & Francis.

Kling, C.A., Hyde, J.S., Showers, C.J., & Buswell, B.N. (1999). Gender differences in self-esteem: A meta-analysis. *Psychological Bulletin, 125*(4), 470–500.

Komar, A.A. (1994). Adolescent school crises: Structure, issues and techniques for postventions. *International Journal of Adolescence & Youth, 5*, 35–46.

Larson, M., & Sweeten, G. (2012). Breaking up is hard to do: Romantic dissolution, offending, and substance use during the transition to adulthood. *Criminology, 50*(3), 605–636.

Lattanzi-Licht, M. (1996). Helping families with adolescents cope with loss. In C.A Corr & D.E. Balk (Eds.), *Handbook of adolescent death and bereavement* (pp. 219–234). New York: Springer.

Lee, J.A.B., & Swenson, C.R. (2005). Mutual aid: A buffer against risk. In A. Gitterman & L. Shulman (Eds.), *Mutual aid groups, vulnerable & resilient populations, and the life cycle* (pp. 573–596). New York: Columbia University Press.

Lewis, L., & Langer, K.C. (1994). Symbolization in psychotherapy with patients who are disabled. *Journal of Psychotherapy, 48*(2), 231–239.

Lopez, C., & Bhat, C.S. (2007). Supporting students with incarcerated parents in schools: A group intervention. *The Journal for Specialists in Group Work, 32*(2), 139–153.

Low, N., Dugas, E., O'Loughlin, E., Rodriguez, D., Contreras, G., Chaiton, M., & O'Loughlin, J. (2012). Common stressful life events and difficulties are associated with mental health symptoms and substance use in young adults. *BMC Psychiatry, 12*, 1–10.

Luecken, L.J., & Appelhans, B. (2005). Information-processing biases in young adults from bereaved and divorced families. *Journal of Abnormal Psychology, 114*(2), 309–313.

Lurie, C. (1993). *The death of friends vs. family members in late adolescence: The role of perceived social support and self-worth.* (Unpublished master's thesis, Colorado State University, Fort Collins).

Malekoff, A. (2004). *Group work with adolescents: Principles and practice.* New York: Guilford Press.

Malone, P.A. (2007). The impact of peer death on adolescent girls: A task-oriented group intervention. *Journal of Social Work in End-of-Life & Palliative Care, 3*(3), 23–37.

Malone, P.A. (2010). *The impact of peer death on adolescent girls: An efficacy study of the Adolescent Grief and Loss group.* (Doctoral dissertation, The University of Texas at Austin). Retrieved from catalog.lib.utexas.edu.

Malone, P.A. (2011). Children and adolescents growing up in the shadow of divorce. In E.C. Pomeroy & R.B. Garcia (Eds.), *Children and loss: A practical handbook for professionals* (pp. 62–92). Chicago: Lyceum Books.

Malone, P.A. (2012). The impact of peer death on adolescent girls: An efficacy study of the Adolescent Grief and Loss group. *Social Work with Groups, 35*, 35–29.

Malone, P.A., Garcia, R.B., & Pomeroy, E.C. (2011). Children and youth in crisis. In E.C. Pomeroy & R.B. Garcia (Eds.), *Children and loss: A practical handbook for professionals* (pp. 145–168). Chicago: Lyceum Books.

Malone, P.A., Pomeroy, E.C., & Jones, B.L. (2011). Disoriented grief: A lens through which to view the experience of Katrina evacuees. *Journal of Social Work in End-of-Life and Palliative Care, 7*, 241–262.

Martin, T.L. (2002). Disenfranchising the brokenhearted. In K.J. Doka (Ed.), *Disenfranchised grief: New directions, challenges, and strategies for practice* (pp. 233–250). Champaign, IL: Research Press.

Masten, A., Best, K., & Garmezy, N. (1991). Resilience and development: Contributions from the study of children who overcome adversity. *Development and Psychopathology, 2*, 425–444.

McEachern, A.G., & Kenny, M.C. (2007). Transition groups for high school students with disabilities. *The Journal for Specialists in Group Work, 32*(2), 165–177.

McFerran, K., Roberts, M., & O'Grady, L. (2010). Music therapy with bereaved teenagers: A mixed methods perspective. *Death Studies, 34*, 541–565.

McNeil, J.N., Silliman, B., & Swihart, J.J. (1991). Helping adolescents cope with the death of a peer: A high school case study. *Journal of Adolescent Research, 6*, 132–145.

Melhem, N.M., Day, N., Shear, M.K., Day, R., Reynolds, C.F., & Brent, D. (2004). Traumatic grief among adolescents exposed to a peer's suicide. *American Journal of Psychiatry, 161*, 1411–1416.

Meyers, B. (2002). Disenfranchised grief and the loss of an animal companion. In K.J. Doka (Ed.), *Disenfranchised grief: New directions, challenges, and strategies for practice* (pp. 251–264). Champaign, IL: Research Press.

Midgley, E.K., & Lo, C.C. (2013). The role of a parent's incarceration in the emotional health and problem behaviors of at-risk adolescents. *Journal of Child & Adolescent Substance Abuse, 22*, 85–103.

Monroe, S.M., Rohde, P., Seeley, J.R., & Lewinsohn, P.M. (1999). Life events and depression in adolescence: Relationship loss as a prospective risk factor for first onset of major depressive disorder. *Journal of Abnormal Psychology, 108*(4), 606–614.

Montgomery, A. (2013). *Neurobiology essentials for clinicians*. New York: Norton.

Moss, J. (2012). What's in a name? In R.A. Neimeyer (Ed.), *Techniques of grief therapy: Creative practices for counseling the bereaved*. New York: Routledge.

Moss, M. (2004). Grief on the Web. *OMEGA, 49*(1), 77–81.

Natsuaki, M.N., Biehl, M.C., & Ge, X.J. (2009). Trajectories of depressed mood from early adolescence to young adulthood: The effects of pubertal timing and adolescent dating. *Journal of Research on Adolescence, 19*(1), 47–74.

Neimeyer, R.A. (2012). Chair work. In R.A. Neimeyer (Ed.), *Techniques of grief therapy: Creative practices for counseling the bereaved* (pp. 266–273). New York: Routledge.

Neimeyer, R.A., & Jordan, J.R. (2002). Disenfranchisement as empathic failure: Grief therapy and the co-construction of meaning. In K.A. Doka (Ed.), *Disenfranchised grief: New directions, challenges, and strategies for practice* (pp. 95–118). Champaign, IL: Research Press.

Nichols, E.B., & Loper, A.B. (2012). Incarceration in the household: Academic outcomes of adolescents with incarcerated household members. *Journal of Youth and Adolescence, 41*, 1455–1471.

Nikels, H.J., Mims, G.A., & Mims, M.J. (2007). Allies against hate: A school-based diversity sensitivity training experience. *The Journal for Specialists in Group Work, 32*(2), 126–138.

Noppe, I.C., & Noppe, L.D. (1997). Evolving meanings of death during early, middle, and later adolescence. *Death Studies, 21*, 253–275.

Noppe, I.C., & Noppe, L.D. (2004). Adolescent experiences with death: Letting go of immortality. *Journal of Mental Health Counseling, 26*(2), 146–167.

Noppe, I.C., & Noppe, L.D. (2008). When a friend dies. In K.J. Doka & A.S. Tucci (Eds.), *Living with grief: Children and adolescents* (pp. 175–192). Washington, DC: Hospice Foundation of America.

O'Brien, J.M., Goodenow, C., & Espin, O. (1991). Adolescents' reactions to the death of a peer. *Adolescence, 26*(102), 431–440.

O'Conner, D.L. (2002). Toward empowerment: Re-visioning family support groups. *Social Work with Groups, 25*(4), 37–46.

Oltjenbruns, K.A. (1996). Death of a friend during adolescence: Issues and impacts. In C.A. Corr & D.E. Balk (Eds.), *Handbook of adolescent death and bereavement* (pp. 196–216). New York: Springer.

Oransky, M., & Maracek, J. (2009). "I'm not going to be a girl": Masculinity and emotions in boys' friendships and peer groups. *Journal of Adolescent Research, 24*, 218–241.

Paisley, P.O., & Milsom, A. (2007). Group work as an essential contribution to transforming school counseling. *The Journal for Specialists in Group Work, 32*(1), 9–17.

Pennebaker, J.W., Zech, E., & Rime, B. (2001). Disclosing and sharing emotions: Psychological, social, and health consequences. In M.S. Stroebe, R.O. Hansson, W. Stroebe, & H. Schut (Eds.), *Handbook of bereavement research: Consequences, coping, and care* (pp. 517–544). Washington, DC: American Psychological Association.

Pesek, E.M. (2002). The role of support groups in disenfranchised grief. In K.J. Doka (Ed.), *Disenfranchised grief: New directions, challenges, and strategies for practice* (pp. 127–134). Champaign, IL: Research Press.

Petersen, S., Bull, C., Propst, O., Dettinger, S., & Detwiler, L. (2005). Narrative therapy to prevent illness-related stress disorder. *Journal of Counseling & Development, 83*, 41–47.

Phillips, S.D., Burns, B.J., Wagner, H.R., Kramer, T.L., & Robbins, J.M. (2002). Parental incarceration among adolescents receiving mental health services. *Journal of Child and Family Studies, 11*(4), 3385–3399.

Potash, J.S., & Handel, S. (2012). Memory boxes. In R.A. Neimeyer (Ed.), *Techniques of grief therapy: Creative practices for counseling the bereaved* (pp. 243–246). New York: Routledge.

Pynoos, R.S., Steinberg, A.M., & Goenjian, A. (1996). Traumatic stress in childhood and adolescence: Recent developments and current controversies. In B.A. van der Kolk, A.C. McFarlane, & L. Weisaeth (Eds.), *Traumatic stress: The effects of overwhelming experience on mind, body, and society* (pp. 331–358). New York: The Guilford Press.

Rando, T.A. (1993). *Treatment of complicated mourning.* Champaign, IL: Research Press.

Rask, K., Kaunonen, M., & Paunonen-Ilmonen, M. (2002). Adolescent coping with grief after the death of a loved one. *International Journal of Nursing Practice, 8,* 137–142.

Rheingold, A.A., Smith, D.W., Ruggiero, K.J., Saunders, B.E., Kilpatrick, D.G., & Resnick, H.S. (2004). Loss, trauma, exposure, and mental health in a representative sample of 12–17 year-old youth: Data from the National Survey of Adolescents. *Journal of Loss and Trauma, 9*(1), 10–19.

Rickgarn, R.L.V. (1987). The death response team: Responding to the forgotten grievers. *Journal of Counseling and Development, 66,* 197–199.

Rickgarn, R.L.V. (1996). The need for postvention on college campuses: A rationale and case study findings. In C.A. Corr & D.E. Balk (Eds.), *Handbook of adolescent death and bereavement* (pp. 273–292). New York: Springer.

Ringler, L.L., & Hayden, D.C. (2000). Adolescent bereavement and social support: Peer loss compared to other losses. *Journal of Adolescent Research, 15*(2), 209–230.

Rittner, B., & Smyth, N.J. (1999). Time-limited cognitive-behavioral group interventions with suicidal adolescents. *Social Work with Groups, 22*(2/3), 55–75.

Roberts, P. (2004). The living and the dead: Community in the virtual cemetery. *OMEGA, 49*(1), 57–76.

Rose, A.J., & Rudolph, K.D. (2006). A review of sex differences in peer relationship processes: Potential trade-offs for the emotional and behavioral development of girls and boys. *Psychological Bulletin, 132*(1), 98–131.

Rosen, H. (1991). Child and adolescent bereavement. *Child and Adolescent Social Work, 8*(1), 5–16.

Rothschild, B. (2000). *The body remembers: The physiology of trauma and trauma treatment.* New York: Norton.

Rowling, L. (2002). Youth and disenfranchised grief. In K.J. Doka (Ed.), *Disenfranchised grief: New directions, challenges, and strategies for practice* (pp. 275–292). Champaign, IL: Research Press.

Rush, C.M., & Akos, P. (2007). Supporting children and adolescents with deployed caregivers: A structured group approach for school counselors. *The Journal for Specialists in Group Work, 32*(2), 113–125.

Saltzman, W.R., Layne, C.M., & Pynoos, R.S. (2002). A developmental approach to school-based treatment of adolescents exposed to trauma and traumatic loss. *Journal of Child and Adolescent Group Therapy, 11*(2/3), 43–56.

Saltzman, W.R., Steinberg, A.M., Layne, C.M., Aisenberg, E., & Pynoos, R.S. (2001). A developmental approach to school-based treatment of adolescents exposed to trauma and traumatic loss. *Journal of Child and Adolescent Group Therapy, 11*(2/3), 43–56.

Schachter, S. (1991). Adolescent experiences with the death of a peer. *OMEGA, 24,* 1–11.

Schut, J., Stroebe, M.S., van den Bout, J., & Terheggen, M. (2001). The efficacy of bereavement interventions: Determining who benefits. In M.S. Stroebe, R.O. Hansson, W. Stroebe, & H. Schut (Eds.), *Handbook of bereavement research: Consequences, coping, and care* (pp. 705–738). Washington, DC: American Psychological Association.

Schuurman, D. (2008). Grief groups for grieving children and adolescents. In K.J. Doka & A.S. Tucci (Eds.), *Living with grief: Children and adolescents* (pp. 255–268). Washington, DC: Hospice Foundation of America.

Servaty, H.L., & Hayslip, B. (2001). Adjustment to loss among adolescents. *OMEGA, 43*(4), 311–330.

Servaty-Seib, H.L. (2009). Death of a friend during adolescence. In D.E. Balk & C.A. Corr (Eds.), *Adolescent encounters with death, bereavement, and coping* (pp. 217–235). New York: Springer Publishing.

Shaller, J., & Smith, C.R. (2002). Music therapy with adolescents experiencing loss. *The Forum, 28*(1), 2–4.

Shulman, L. (1985/86). The dynamics of mutual aid. *Social Work with Groups, 8*(4), 51–60.

Shulman, L. (1999). *The skills of helping: Individuals, families, groups, and communities.* Itasca, IL: Peacock.

Shulman, L. (2005). Healing the hurts: A short-term group for separated, widowed, and divorced single parents. In A. Gitterman & L. Shulman (Eds.), *Mutual aid groups, vulnerable & resilient populations, and the life cycle* (pp. 448–468). New York: Columbia University Press.

Shulman, L. (2006). *The skills of helping individuals, families, groups, and communities.* Belmont, CA: Thomson Brooks/Cole.

Siegel, D.J. (1999). *The developing mind: Toward a neurobiology of interpersonal experience.* New York: Guilford Press.

Siegel, D.J. (2011). *Mindsight: The new science of personal transformation.* New York: Bantam Books.

Siegel, D.J. (2013). *Brainstorm: The power and purpose of the teenage brain.* New York: Penguin.

Sklar, F. (1991). Grief as a family affair: Property rights, grief rights, and the exclusion of close friends as survivors. *OMEGA: The Journal of Death and Dying, 24*(2), 109–121.

Sklar, F., & Hartley, S.F. (1990). Close friends as survivors: Bereavement patterns in a "hidden" population. *OMEGA: The Journal of Death and Dying, 21*(2), 103–112.

Sofka, C.J. (1997). Social support "internetworks," caskets for sale, and more. Thanatology and the information superhighway. *Death Studies, 21*(6), 553–574.

Sofka, C.J. (2009). Adolescents, technology, and the Internet: Coping with loss in the digital world. In D.E. Balk & C.A. Corr (Eds.), *Adolescent encounters with death, bereavement, and coping* (pp. 155–173). New York: Springer Publishing.

Steese, S., Dollette, M., Phillips, W., Hossfeld, E., Matthews, G., & Taormina, G. (2006). Understanding Girls' Circle as an intervention on perceived social support, body image, self-efficacy, locus of control, and self-esteem. *Adolescence, 41*(161), 55–74.

Stevenson, R.G. (2002). Sudden death in schools. In K.J. Doka (Ed.), *Disenfranchised grief: New directions, challenges, and strategies for practice* (pp. 194–213). Champaign, IL: Research Press.

Stevenson, R.G. (2008). Helping students cope with grief. In K.J. Doka & A.S. Tucci (Eds.), *Living with grief: Children and adolescents* (pp. 317–334). Washington, DC: Hospice Foundation of America.

Stroebe, M., & Schut, H. (1999). The dual process model of coping with bereavement: Rationale and description. *Death Studies, 23*(3), 197–225.

Stroebe, M., & Schut, H. (2001). Meaning making in the dual process model of coping with bereavement. In R.A. Neimeyer (Ed.), *Meaning reconstruction & the experience of loss* (pp. 55–73). Washington, DC: American Psychological Association.

Strouse, S. (2014). Collage: Integrating the torn pieces. In B.E. Thompson & R.A. Neimeyer (Eds.), *Grief and the expressive arts: Practices for creating meaning* (pp. 187–197). New York: Routledge.

Subrahmanyam, K., & Greenfield, P. (2008). Online communication and adolescent relationships. *The Future of Children, 18*(1), 119–146.

Tedeschi, R.G. (1996). Support groups for bereaved adolescents. In C.A. Corr & D.E. Balk (Eds.), *Handbook of adolescent death and bereavement* (pp. 293–311). New York: Springer.

Tillitski, C.J. (1990). A meta-analysis of estimated effect sizes for group versus individual versus control treatments. *International Journal of Group Psychotherapy, 40*(2), 215–224.

Tuckman, B. (1965). Developmental sequences in small groups. *Psychological Bulletin, 63,* 384–399.

Tyson-Rawson, K.J. (1996). Adolescent responses to the death of a parent. In C.A. Corr & D.E. Balk (Eds.), *Handbook of adolescent death and bereavement* (pp. 155–172). New York: Springer.

U.S. Bureau of the Census. (2012). www.census.gov.

Valentine, L. (1996). Professional interventions to assist adolescents who are coping with death and bereavement. In C.A. Corr & D.E. Balk (Eds.), *Handbook of adolescent death and bereavement* (pp. 312–328). New York: Springer.

van der Kolk, B. (2014). *The body keeps the score. Brain, mind, and body in the healing of trauma*. New York: Viking.

Vanderwerker, L., & Prigerson, H. (2004). Social support and technical connectedness as protective factors in bereavement. *Journal of Loss and Trauma, 1*, 45–57.

van Dijck, J. (2013). *The culture of connectivity: A critical history of social media*. London: Oxford University Press.

Wallerstein, J., & Lewis, J. (2004). The unexpected legacy of divorce. *Psychoanalytic Psychology, 21*(3), 353–370.

Way, N. (2011). *Deep secrets: Boys' friendships and the crisis of connection*. Cambridge, MA: Harvard University Press.

Webb, L., & Brigman, G.A. (2007). Student success skills: A structured group intervention for school counselors. *The Journal for Specialists in Group Work, 32*(2), 190–201.

Webb, N.B. (2002). Traumatic death of a friend/peer: Case of Susan, age 9. In N.B. Webb (Ed.), *Helping bereaved children: A handbook for practitioners* (pp. 167–193). New York: Guilford Press.

Wlodarczyk, N. (2014). Lyric analysis. In B.E. Thompson & R.A. Neimeyer (Eds.), *Grief and the expressive arts: Practices for creating meaning* (pp. 47–49). New York: Routledge.

Worden, J., & Silverman, P. (1996). Parental death and the adjustment of school-age children. *OMEGA, 33*(2), 91–102.

Worden, J.W., & Winokuer, H.R. (2011). A task-based approach for counseling the bereaved. In R.A. Neimeyer, D.L. Harris, H.R. Winokuer, & G.F. Thornton (Eds.), *Grief and bereavement in contemporary society: Bridging research and practice* (pp. 57–67). New York: Routledge.

Yalom, I.D. (1970). *The theory and practice of group psychotherapy*. New York: Basic Books.

Yalom, I.D., & Leszcz, M. (2005). *The theory and practice of group psychotherapy* (5th ed.). New York: Basic Books.

Ziffer, J.M., Crawford, E., & Penney-Wietor, J. (2007). The boomerang bunch: A school-based multifamily group approach for students and their families recovering from parental separation and divorce. *The Journal for Specialists in Group Work, 32*(2), 154–164.

INDEX

continuity, rituals of 131–2
coping: Adolescent Grief and Loss
    (AGL) group 123, 124, 125–8;
    group therapy, 98, 107
crying: loss, grief or trauma 24–5
culture: adolescent's grief 73

D

death: of friend or peer 12, 56–8; of
    friend or peer by suicide
    59–60; of grandparent 51–2;
    loss, grief or trauma 25–6;
    loss during adolescence
    47; of parent 47–51; of pet
    55–6; in school 60–1; of
    sibling 52–5
de-idealization of parents 34
deidentification 36
de-stress 107
disenfranchisement: death of friend
    or peer 58; friendship loss
    42; grief xv–xvi, 29–30;
    romantic breakup 43, 45
divorce, parental 32–5
drawing therapy 109–10

E

early adolescence 2–5; cognitive
    development 4–5; emotional
    development 4; physical
    development 3; social
    development 3–4
eating 16, 18–19, 83, 105, 107
email 85, 88
emotional development: early
    adolescence 4; late
    adolescence 7–8
emotional responses: loss, grief, and
    trauma 16, 23–6, 138
empty chair therapy 147–8
existential factors 115, 116, 120

F

Facebook 23, 24; adolescents on 85–6;
    benefits of 87–8; risk of 89;
    virtual grave marker 93–5

family connection, grieving adolescents
    71–3
family reenactment 114, 116, 119
fight, flight, or freeze response 23–4,
    81, 83
financial issues, relocation due to 38–9
Flickr 85
friends: death by suicide 59–60, 67,
    89; death of 56–8; grieving
    adolescents 73–4
friendships: adolescent boys 65–6;
    adolescent girls 63–5; loss of
    40–2
funeral ritual 130–1

G

gender differences: adolescent boy
    relationships 65–6; adolescent
    girl relationships 63–5;
    grieving style 66–70; group
    therapy 101–3; socialization
    63, 67–8, 70
Gestalt therapy 147–8
goodbye 76, 94, 130, 131
grandparents, death of 51–2
grave marker, Facebook as virtual 93–5
gray, shades of 5, 40
grief, disenfranchised 29–30
grieving: gender differences 66–70;
    influences on style 69–70;
    instrumental style 69;
    intuitive style 68; tasks in
    process of 91–2
grieving adolescents: family
    connection for 71–3;
    friends and peers 73–4;
    psychoeducation 74–7;
    symptom management
    77–84; see also symptom
    management
grounding techniques 77, 79–80, 83,
    123, 143
group cohesiveness 115, 120
group interventions: Adolescent
    Group and Loss (AGL)
    group model 118–19;
    interactional groups 113–16;

mutual aid groups 116–18; mutual aid processes 120–2; structure of AGL group 122–8; therapeutic factors of AGL group 119–20

group therapy 97–101; activities 106–11; adolescent boys' group 102–3; adolescent girls' group 102; affirmations 108; coed adolescent groups 101–2; coping strategies 107; effectiveness of adolescent groups 100; finding benefit in 110–11; helpful and hurtful words 109; icebreakers 106–7; individual therapy and 100–1; journaling and drawing 109–10; participation 97, 98; private therapy practice offices 105–6; school settings 103–5; stress relievers 107; support identification 108–9; telling the story 107–8

H

healing light relaxation technique 78
hope, instillation and maintenance of 114, 119
Hopkins Symptom Checklist 48
hypervigilance 10

I

icebreaker 106–7
imitative behavior 114, 119
incarceration of parent: non-death loss 35–7
Instagram 74, 85
instrumental grieving style, adolescent boys 69
interactional groups 113–16; therapeutic factors 114–16
interpersonal learning 115, 116, 120
intervention see group therapy; therapy
intuitive grieving style, adolescent girls 68

J

journaling, therapy 109–10, 142

L

label/labeling 24, 65, 102
late adolescence: cognitive development 8–9; emotional development 7–8; physical development 5–6; social development 6–7
loss see non-death loss
Loss History Timeline 142–5

M

mementos 148
memory box 148–9
model: Adolescent Grief and Loss (AGL) group 118–19; coping 70, 72
music connection with adolescents 140–2
mutual aid groups: intervention 116, 118; processes 117, 120–2
mutual demand 117, 121
mutual support 117, 118–19, 121
MySpace 85, 90

N

narrative construction, loss, grief, and trauma 134–6
National Longitudinal Survey of Adolescent Health 59
natural disaster, relocation due to 39–40
non-death loss 31–2; friendship loss 40–2; incarceration of parent 35–7; parental divorce 32–5; relocation 37–40; romantic breakup 42–5
nonlethal self-injury 97, 105, 143–5

O

over-functioning role, coping 50

P

parent: death of 47–51; divorce of 32–5; employment relocation 38; incarceration 35–7